HUSTLE 4 HAPPINESS

A Decades Walk

HUSTLE 4 HAPPINESS

A Decades Walk

Mohamad-Nawaf Taleb

(Shadi's Brother)

TABLE OF CONTENTS

Foreword

June 21, 1993 was the day that began the journey of finding the reason behind my existence. Once an only child, life changed as I became an older brother in '93 when Shadi was born. The feeling of how precious life was with him was realized when I became an only child again on January 24, 2011.

Shadi, my brother, was born in Mississauga at Trillium Hospital and lived to tell the tale of a 17-year-old living in a suburban city, born to immigrant parents from Lebanon who had left everything behind to come to Canada and provide a better future for their unborn children. My father had left my mother when I was just 10 days old to migrate to Canada; we did not see him again until I was 13 months old. He left a war-torn country alone, got stranded in Sweden, and then arrived in Canada to start this better life. He landed in 1990 at Toronto Pearson Airport and decided that Mississauga was the place to call home. My mother and I immigrated to reunite with him. Life, as I recall, was normal, but what is normal to a child?

In 1993, Shadi was born at Trillium Hospital on June 21, the first day of summer. We called him "the summer baby" and "the good luck charm," as he was always celebrating his birthday in the best of weather. He was a great kid growing up and never really gave my mom any trouble other than the occasional smart trades he'd make with me, and I'd whine about it. The kid was always ahead of his time even when he was just 4 years old. At that age, my father decided to go back to Lebanon for a few years, and we all went back with him.

During this time, we grew into each other, becoming best friends. We shared the same bus to school and back. During our lunches, I would go see him, and he would come to the metal fence where I would give him lunch money if he needed it. The truth is that even at that age his charm had allowed him to develop a following of students who reported to him and gave him snacks and lunch in exchange for being in his kindergarten group. He was a strategist even at a young age, placing his hands in all the available pots so that he could take care of those around him. Mind you, he would take the snacks and disperse them to those who didn't have anything, making sure everyone had a piece to eat.

In 2001, a few months before September 11, we came back home to Mississauga. The family had fallen on hard times, and the parents had made the decision to come back. It was then that we were introduced to the Canadian schools. Once again, we had a four-year age gap, which unfortunately meant that we were never able to go to the same school at the same time again, but that didn't matter—we were brothers. He was able to learn from others around him and to gauge his surroundings to learn the best knowledge and apply it within his everyday life.

One story that was told to me not too long ago is that while waiting for the bus under our old building, he approached a kid out of nowhere and just started speaking to him. He made him guess his name by saying things like, "Who's the real slim?" From that day, they waited for the bus together for the whole year. His friend recalled that to this day, he has not met anyone with people skills like Shadi's; he was so gentle and trustworthy. From someone who met another kid at a bus station to having his friend tell his legacy forever—that was the type of young man my brother was.

2

He grew into this wonder that everyone around him would gravitate toward, not knowing why but rather just being attracted to him. We shared a lot in common, however he was his own man at such a young age. He achieved a lot by 17, and his mind was one of them. Moving back into the area we lived in when we first came into the country allowed him to flourish and to make friends who would become legacy-holders later on.

Attending the Valleys public school in Mississauga, he was friends with everyone, and everyone knew him, from the family to the people down the street. The boy was cute. There wasn't a girl his age who didn't have googly eyes for him, and that got me JEALOUS!

Together, we made music. I introduced him to making music. I always had a knack for finding out how things were made, and I loved music. Slowly, he learned the behind-the-scenes process of putting a song together and listened closely to how the main structure of a song works. Before I could even get it right, this kid was 10 steps ahead of me. The first song we recorded together was "My Girl," and he dedicated a part of it to his girl at the time. If there was ever a part of a music program that I couldn't figure out, I'd leave it to him for an hour, and he'd come back with it fixed. He was the go-to, the fixer, the guy you can depend on. I lived 17 years of my life knowing I had a brother in the flesh, someone to go to and someone to depend on. He really was someone who always had your back and kept it tight when the times got tough.

Before I conclude my thoughts on the reason behind this book, there is a story I want to share with you: while in high school, Shadi's friend at another high school messaged him, and as they were talking, he had mentioned that he didn't have his lunch. Without hesitation, my brother went to the other school and gave him money to buy lunch and then went back to his school. He never asked for anything in return but rather wanted to help his friend out.

From being an older brother to becoming an only child, life hasn't been easy. From losing my best friend to becoming my own best friend, life hasn't been easy. He was truly an inspiration and a constant motivation for me to become great.

My brother till this day is my brother and is still teaching me valuable lessons. He was an individual who was and is still being spoken of. The reason I write this book is for ***him***, to showcase the aftereffects on my life and how I got through it in hopes of helping someone who is going through the struggle without having the courage to speak out.

Thank you, Shadi.

Preface

Why this book? What's in it for me, or better yet, what's in it for you?

There are multiple people who will give you different answers as to why I wrote this book or what encompassed my aura that allowed me to write this. Let me tell you firsthand that the intention of this book is pure and is the derivative of humility and love from the depths of my heart. I was built by those around me and the surroundings that influenced my truest of being. Hence, I write to you, the reader, my experiences and what had helped overcome the tragedies, stress, depression, anxiety, and much more.

This book is a firsthand look at situations that I have faced and how I came to conquer every problem, from relationships to career moves and the negativity that comes with every situation. When I started this book in 2016 it was out of the purity of helping others through my rough ideas of life. Now that I am continuously updating this book, I find that I am helping myself as well.

All my life I have been the subject of bullying, racism, and inconsistency; that has led to my being volatile. I wanted to take my past dealings, my present situation, and my future outlook in translation and provide it to you, the reader, in hopes of connecting with someone who needs help.

Human beings by nature do not open up and the will to speak at times is silenced. Through my vulnerability, I wanted to open up to everyone about the issues I faced with the hope of making a possible connection to you. Through the experience of pain, heartbreak, depression, stress, social anxiety, and much more, I wanted to share my experience of overcoming such tragedies so that this may act as a tool that may help you overcome your own situation.

For those who are solid and believe that they are not in need of help, I commend you. Let this be an insight into the human struggle of what was and what is. Frankly, simply living is not a life worth dying for, however, purposeful living is one worth ten thousand deaths.

I had many acquaintances during the years it took me to put this book together, and through them, I gained experience and knowledge. Among my many iterations of daily activities, I was able to help myself revert back to the text written and that, in essence, helped me regain consciousness. I began living a simple yet comfortable life where stagnancy became my best friend and improvement became my worst enemy. I should've kept my enemy close, but I decided to embody my friendship with comfort. This comfort brought on many things such as depression, anxiety, and social dilemmas.

You will find that in this book I have written about the art of the hustle risk, positivity, mental health, depression, the way to overcome social anxiety, and much more. My goal was to write this in a raw and very personal way, shedding light on real life experiences, so that you can all connect with me. I hope I succeeded in that aspect.

While writing, I read a few books that were able to help me gain consciousness, books on ideologies that I also applied in real life. Mind you, I really went through this; none of it was experimental. My love, my struggle, and my recovery were all about honesty and despair.

I don't think that there is a better time to reveal this project and book to the world than now. With how 2020 has affected everyone and how we have all taken a step back, it is most important that we stand unified as a human race to solidify mental health and boost our systems together. If you are struggling, as I know many of us are, I ask that you use this book to your advantage so that you can become better again. Please know that there are other people out there that are suffering just like you; it is okay to feel the way you are feeling. Allow this book to build a connection with you on a deeper and more intimate level of energy. I want this book to make you better, and if you are already good, then to become even better. The foundation of what you rely on will change, and it is up to you to enforce it with every ounce of strength you can muster. The physical body is connected to your mental health in ways that cannot be identified. One thing for certain is that if you keep your physical side up to date, your mental side surely follows. Many go along in life without realizing that most of us are fighting internal struggles, so it's important to be your own author of the nonjudgmental book in your life.

That is the goal of this book. Even if only 5% of this book has helped, then I am a happy human. If none of it has helped, I apologize and would love to hear your story as to what I can do to help. If I have touched your heart, please send this to a friend if they need it as well. Together, we can change the world, one heart at a time.

God bless, and may you enjoy the rest of this passage.

CHAPTER 1

Real 2 Hustle & Hustle 2 Real

Every day I wake up and start my hustle. Whether it is with work, food prep, gym prep or my mental prep, I hustle to live that day. The nature of the life is that it is a hustle. According to the dictionary, the word hustle means "obtain by forceful action or persuasion;" however, it could be defined in your own way. The most basic form of hustle is getting out of bed. The hustle in the morning is the most important. For me when it comes to getting myself ready for the day, I need to hustle out the bed first. Some hustles are more tiring than others. My mental anxiety, stemming from the accident in 2011, is my greatest of hustles that I work with on a daily and hourly basis. Through the years, I have heard individuals tell me that going through that type of tragedy

9

must have been the worst thing ever, and that it gets easier as you go on. The truth is that you end up facing your own worst demons, and it never gets better; you just learn how to live with it and hustle on with your life. That is part of my daily hustle, to adapt to the new lifestyle I have been given. Not a minute or a second go by when I don't find myself fighting the urge to stop remembering events of the accident my family and I went through.

At times the hustle is real and at times, the real becomes the hustle. You may think this is confusing but let me break it down for you. In certain instances, I find myself hustling to stay motivated and to learn how to constantly remain positive when flashbacks or the even the smallest of things set me off. The hustle here is to keep myself going and to take my mind of off things; this is not always successful. That hustle stems from me hustling to find an alternative to take me out of the black hole I fall into. Whether it is switching my routine to a new one or going out of my way to buy a chocolate bar (which always places me in an utter utopia), I force myself to hustle out of that negative mood. As a man there isn't much that can get me out of my own little bubble when I start dwelling deep in the black abyss, but it's important for anyone to find out what makes them happy and hustle for it. This is where the hustle is real and is where I find myself the most tired.

As for when the real becomes the hustle, this is more of an uncontrollable situation. Throughout the years, my way of dealing with things has changed. The accident placed us (my family) through instances that we never thought could be repeated or were never accustomed to. Maybe you as the reader, can relate but here's an example of what I mean when I say the real becomes the hustle. After the accident we were required to go to court on multiple occasions for the trial, and that we were never used to. During the 10 years of us attending court, we kept on hustling our thoughts out of that reality into a more positive one.

Certain situations in life that we usually never imagine we'd have to go through push us into hustling our efforts and energy into maintaining what we see as normal. No one is born into a perfect life, and essentially no one lives a perfect life either. From the moment we are born we are susceptible to mistakes, anger, frustration, sins, lies, bad decisions, good decisions, and uncontrollable instances. The realities of our choices have consequences, regardless of the severity. The consequences can either be positive or negative. The reality that stems from both creates a new reality and a path that never existed, and we are usually left asking, "How do I deal with this now?" Well, the answer is that there really isn't anyone out there to tell you how to hustle yourself out of the reality of the situation you are currently in. How you deal with it depends on how you want to see yourself dealing with it.

We fall into the habit of living lucid dreams during the day and dreaming of an alternate life at night. It could never be what I wanted it to be, and by "it" I mean the way my days flowed. The worst part of going through my day is waking up to realize I need to start the hustle all over again. A little insight on my life may give you the energy you need to motivate yourself to get better and find what works for you. I am very organized and find myself in a place of repetition that is continuously having new add-ons, so that when I wake up, I tend to look out the window to check the weather. At one point of my life after the accident I found myself looking out the window and cursing waking up because I hated waking up without him. I would literally wake up, sit on the edge of my bed and utter, "F*** this." That part of the hustle came to me naturally, I needed to get out of my own deep black hole that circumstances placed me in, but instead I dug myself in deeper. I didn't have the chance to bounce back the whole time I was in the hole. After I looked out the window, the next part of my hustle was getting out of bed and starting my day.

(Side note: I just poured myself a double shot of Virginia Black [thought I'd try it out] and put on *Sidewalks* by The Weekend to help me get into my zone. I need to be zoned to speak my truest of self to you, so that you receive nothing but true authenticity.)

The moment I get out of bed, I walk out of my room to go into the washroom, and I am immediately reminded of the missing piece in my life as I pass my brother's room. That split 3-second window into looking into how my life was completely throws me into a loop, which leaves me trying to pick up the pieces and recuperate for the rest of the morning. As I get dressed, I am then hustling my way out of what could have been to what is now, and I allow reality to set back in, the hustle becomes real, again. While looking at myself in the mirror it all sets in. I am reminded of who I am and what I am capable off.

Looking at yourself in the mirror and allowing yourself the time to look into your own reflection will help you. The deep appreciation of your own beauty will strike you from time to time, and the real now becomes the hustle. Looking at myself, or into myself, in the mirror allows me to realize the resemblance to my past, my future, and most importantly the present moment.

I encourage you to try it, to take the time out of your day to walk over to a mirror and isolate yourself from everyone.

Look into the mirror and allow yourself to have a minute of silence and reflection (pun intended) to the point where you begin to see the small details in your face. Think of the past, where you were, and of the present, where you are now. You will slowly begin to realize that all that once existed and bothered you is no longer able to bother you now. Although this reflection may result in a positive outcome, also note that remembering your past may bring up any anger that you may have towards some issues. The trick here is to HUSTLE, AND THE REAL BECOMES THE HUSTLE. Switch that reality that you lived in and currently live in into a positive reflection.

We are not bound by facts but rather by our imagination.

After I get dressed in my bedroom, I end up walking out to the washroom to pass my brother's room again, where I'm reminded of my reality; but now, I've pulled myself into a happy state that makes it easier to remember it, to remember him. The hustle that became so real when I woke up has now become the real that makes me hustle and reminds me of all the reasons I hustled and worked. From then on, I wash up and head downstairs to make myself a cup of green tea to start my day. As the reader, you must know that all I do, and all my actions are part of a reaction that I was once involved in. All my actions have a reason, and I may not say them out loud to the world. but it's a part of me that is beautiful. My green tea is my real becoming my hustle again; it was my brother's favorite drink; hence, I start my day with what means most to me.

Implement in your life the small things that mean most to you, and you will be happy.

This is truly what keeps me hustling and keeps me going. You see, the point of this book isn't to give you a miracle or a life-altering moment that you read about and then decide to change your life. It's to have you relate to someone who has gone through his rough patches and decided to share it with the world in order to impact someone. I want you, as the reader, to be affected by what you read, and hopefully I am able to reach you through different sections of this book.

When thinking about the life that you currently live, it is always important to remember that you are not bound by it. Okay, so some may not agree with me, as the regular belief is you live the life that has been chosen for you or the life that you choose. However, being bound by circumstances will almost never result in any positive outcome unless the individual makes one themselves. It is not strange that as human beings we begin to experience disappointment at a young age; from the time we start walking, to the day we die we will always experience some sort of disappointment. This disappointment could stem from a situation that you have no control over, and this does not make you bound to the details of life. Becoming the hustle, stemming from the real situation that you may be in would be you walking out of the facts that life has dealt you and looking for a better alternative. When I mentioned being bound only by imagination, I truly meant it. The facts are there for you to cry about and stress yourself over regarding the shortcomings of your life, but your imagination is what will allow you to run wild with it.

To give you a quick insight on my life and how I dare to make such a statement: I experienced the loss of my brother at the age of 21. I had to travel overseas with nothing for 2 years and came back to Toronto with nothing other than the $57.00 I had in my bank account. I was of course living with my parents, and they provided me with the necessities to get back on my feet, but if it wasn't for me running with my imagination I would not be here. The fact was that I was broke, dead broke. I had no winter clothes, I had no car to call my own, I had no bed that I was used to, I had no job, and I had no trust in society after being away from it for so long. These exact facts are not there to stick, though, not unless you allow them to. As human beings we are capable of the unexpected if we only truly run with our imagination. I did not want to constantly be the individual with no job, no car, no money, no nice clothes, and I sure did not want to be the individual with no trust in society.

I started to let my mind run. I let it cross oceans in imagination and color.

I started making notes of what I want to be and where I think my reality will be in a few years if I hustle. I started noting things that are materialistic and items that I wanted regardless of what was to happen. I also jotted down the most important things that I truly desired to gain standing in society again, and I promised myself that I would do nothing but work on getting there in 2 years. I gave myself a window and did not shy away from it. I knew for a fact that I did not know how I was going to do it, but I knew then, and I know now, that I will make it happen. It is important to focus on the real things in life that you want to make happen and to

BELIEVE that if you know in the back of your mind what your goal is, and write it down, you will be successful.

A quick reminder: this isn't for anyone thinking, "I'm going to read this, and I'll be good in two years with what I want." No. This is for individuals who want to hustle and no longer be constrained by the facts of life that they have been dealt. It is always important to set life decisions that will impact you in a manner that you did not think of before. Some of the material items that I wanted were a car, new shoes, new jackets, a TV for my room, and a motorcycle. Mind you, they did not happen in that order, but I still made it happen. I knew what car I wanted and what the features were by seeing it online, but what I did next was different. I had bought a car from my dad so that I could call it my own and say, "I have a car," but it wasn't what I wanted. I called a friend of mine and asked him to come with me car shopping, knowing very well that I did not have money for the car; however, I did not say a word to him. We drove around from dealership to dealership until I found the car that I knew I would drive one day. I sat in the car, fixed my seat, opened up the glove box, fixed the radio to what I wanted, and took it for a test drive. I knew right then and there that my imagination had run wild and had me running. With it in front of me I just needed to get it. For the next year or so, I did not have the car, but I worked with the intention of finishing off every day happily and hustling through it to get home.

In December of 2015, I put a down payment on the car that I wanted.

I then went searching for the piece of paper where I wrote down all my goals and finally found it after a week. I opened it and found that I had actually accomplished a lot more than just the vehicle purchase. My hustle became so real that I was living my imagination.

Make a list of things, items, successes, or goals that you want. Write them down on a piece of paper and memorize them if you can. Tuck that piece of paper away somewhere where you know you will forget about it until you truly look for it, and then work away. Always remember that whatever has happened in your life, you are not bound by it. You are truly above it all and can accomplish anything you want if only you place in your heart that you want it. Through my trials and tribulations, I found it best to place things I wanted to become better at in my heart and to follow my heart on the journey of getting it all. Remember that the hustle is beautiful, and the rewards that you reap at the end are worth the wait.

I am not the most successful person out there, but what I can do is tell my story about my reality and the hustle to get out of it. Different strategies and active ways to place yourself first within your circle of life are very important. It is key that you can establish this, and it will not come to you while you sleep. You have to constantly be learning and open to learn more. What we are taught in high school is very primitive (unless you are eventually going for a doctorate or learning how to become an engineer). If, however, you are looking to change the world and make an impact as an entrepreneur, the learning does not stop with high school or the moment you receive your degree. The rebirth in you will happen once you are reborn, and your reality becomes one to touch within your hands.

Rise from the ashes with purpose.

Through my successes, I take hits that sometimes may not be pushing me forward but rather setting me back. This is not a negative situation though, rather just a price that I paid that was not within the educational system. Coming back to Canada with nothing to my name, I knew that my negative situation could only last for so long. My reality was clear, and I had to hustle for what I wanted in the next couple of years. What worked for me was creating short-term and long-term to-do lists. These lists would include goals such as buying a property (long-term), and to achieve this within 5 years I had to put away X dollars every month. This meant cutting back on spending, working more hours, establishing a larger network, and defining where I want to be tomorrow (short-term). They go hand in hand, and neither of them can be achieved alone.

In 2017, I took a $30K hit on a property that I had bought in 2015, and without realizing I was back to where I was in 2014. I was not where I had been 2 years before, rather I had regressed into a situation that existed in 2014. This was not a negative situation; it was impossible that it was all I was going to be. I couldn't accept it for myself, and more importantly I couldn't accept it for my family, period. My reality that I wanted and hustled for just became my new hustle. Taking that kind of hit, as minimal as it could be to others, was huge for me. This is where I applied the rule my grandfather taught and instilled into my brother and me: "If the seas are rough and the wind is not within your favor, adjust your sails".

This was not just a metaphor for a sailor who needed to work around problems but rather a metaphor for us human beings to adjust our sails and move along with the problem. At times, we fight right through the obstacles to a point where we tire ourselves from the stress and issues associated with such rough waves.

When I got the call telling me that I had to dish out $10K for an unexpected issue at my condo, my parents were upset. They were furious, and in all fairness, so was I. I then started to realize the hustle I was so passionately on and became one who had to adjust my patterns of maneuverability.

Simply adjust your mentality.

That was the answer. There was nothing I could do about the fact that I had taken the hit, but instead I could change my outcome. I was placed in a corner. I strongly believe that each and every one of us, when we are placed in a corner, finds that our inner lion or lioness is awoken. We are a primitive race, and if the responsibility outweighs the problem, it becomes reason for us to succeed. My responsibility was making sure I was back on my feet in case anything was to happen to my parents; I would be there for them to fall back on.

You and I are not different. You yourself have that lion in you. Whether you live in the ghetto, whether you are still with your parents, if you're still at your job that you hate, or even if it is a situation that you do not want to be in, be real with yourself. Listen to your surroundings and allow yourself the confidence to realize your reality and to depict the story of how you need to hustle out of it.

Careful though. This does not mean you are running away from your problems (as you should never do) but rather portraying your problems as the reality you are in and accepting the fact that you have one to solve. So, what's next? What do you do after you take the hit?

I didn't make excuses. I was real with my friends and family about my situation, and more importantly, I was honest with myself. I knew that I wasn't going to be able to go shopping and spend the kind of money I had spent when I was up, but I knew that I did it once, and I could do it again. A lot of us go through this exact thing, where we have setbacks and sometimes find ourselves in situations that we never thought we would get back to. The trick isn't to continue living a lavish lifestyle but rather to adapt to what you are currently living with. Taking control of a situation and not allowing this situation to control you really is the aspect we all yearn for. There have been a lot of celebrities and people of power who have hit rock bottom at times but hustled their way out of it. The reality of the situation isn't to remain where you are either but to hustle your way out of it to maintain the status you desire.

The previous text that you have read has brought you into a more intimate portion of my life, an opening, if you will. I really wanted you to understand why I chose this section of my life to talk about and titled it as I did. See growing up, we always knew if we wanted something extravagant, we needed to hustle and get it. Our parents gave us a life they could only dream of when they were young, and for that we are grateful. See we saw it firsthand growing up, the number of hours our parents put in to become successful and pay their bills. My dad had to really hustle his whole life to ensure we had what he wished for as a child.

And 2017 wasn't the only hit that I had taken financially. In 2018 I had a tenant basically walk out on me for 3 to 4 months of rent. After eviction I had tallied up my expenses only to find out I was $15K in the hole, and this wasn't my only hit. I had rented a property to a student who, upon his contract ending, left the country. When I received the key and checked the unit, I had found out that it was also completely destroyed. This left me in another $15K of debt. What a reality that was! These are just some of the hits I took, and not to gloat, but I had to push on through. Seeing how my reality was so financially disabling, I vowed to take control of the hustle I needed to do to get my own version of reality. Head held high, ten toes down, I began hustling my way back to where I needed to be. It was also important that I planned ahead and stayed in front of any curve ball thrown at me.

You see, through my experiences, I hope you find the ability to draw your own conclusions, ideas that can help you finance or hustle your way into any reality that you want. Truly, the 'hustle' isn't specifically tailored to one topic or idea. The hustle is your interpretation of what you want to be better at or become better through. Whether it's relationships, love, career, or even family there is always a different reality waiting for you. At times all it takes is a decision you can make to change the course of your life.

Apart from financials, I know my life isn't 100% complete. I have goals and aspirations that need to be completed at some point in my life. I know you do too, so don't feel left out or left behind. Being motivated to continue the hustle is very difficult nowadays as it requires so much more than mental strength. Talking yourself into the hustle and continuing your day to achieving the results you want requires discipline. You must back your reason for the hustle with discipline and the ability to focus on what is most important to you.

What some of us don't realize is what it takes to hustle in any given subject: you must realize that success comes with sacrifice. The more disciplined you are with achieving the success you want and require, the more you're going to have to give up. Empires were not built overnight, and work doesn't come easy. We have to learn to accept sacrifices. It may make you lonely, but you have to give up something for success.

When it comes to relationships, you must learn that you need to place your significant other first, regardless of the situation. This is the sacrifice you make when you place yourself in a committed relationship. When it's regarding a partnership for a business you must learn that the business comes first prior to anything else in your life. You must cater to the reason you are performing your hustle without compromising your family. This is a balance that will take time to learn and to achieve, however, only you can find it. Your reality may shift; it will change. The end goal must always remain the same. Define the end goal and hustle your way into the reality that you want.

We as a society, living in 2021, worry too much about the opinions of others. The truth is that those who stick to their guns become the reason others celebrate. The journey to hustling your way into the reality that you want isn't easy either. You will receive hate; you will receive love. You will find out some are talking about you. You will also find that those who applaud you are those who talk behind your back. What I am saying is that during your road to the reality you want, you must be disciplined enough to not pay any mind to the external conditions. You really need to focus on what makes the most sense for you without giving anyone an explanation as to why you have chosen that route.

So, what's your current reality?

Have you legitimately sat down and determined how you want to hustle your way out of it? Have you made a checklist? Have you stopped all the outside distractions from entering your life? Most people who say they want to out hustle their reality into another one are doing only half the job. This isn't a time where you do things and stop midway. No. You must place quality into the work you are doing so that you can advance and not double back. The work must be authentic, and you must learn how to cope with the times. If your hustle is real, and you know it, say it with your chest.

If you fall back, that is fine, as long as you know you can continue on the road to your defined success. Nothing can bless you with the outcome you need other than the hard work you place into your life.

Exit Thoughts

I really enjoyed writing this chapter, because it reminded me of situations I always found myself in. It taught me the resiliency I have and how much I can handle. My hustle also showed me how temporary this all is. I learnt that even though pain lasts for a while, it, too, subsides.

At times I found myself hustling my way out of so much. Whether it was love, career, or finances, I always learnt that the word "hustle" gets me to what I want. With hard work and dedication, I was able to overcome my illness in any category that I faced. You have to realize what it is you want to change or develop into in order to create the reality you seek. No one will do it for you, and evidently, no one is willing to help.

I hope I was able to bring you a piece of my hustle and gave you some type of conclusion that you understood. I really attempted to bring you into my small circle of life, so that you can understand all that is going on or went on. The hustle is always going to be involved in your life and whether or not you like it, you must follow it. Do not allow your circumstances to dictate your future. Your vision and hard work will play that role for you. Your surroundings do not dictate who you are either. You better believe it is you that creates your personality and your legacy. Chase that legacy, and do not stop. Allow my story to become motivation for yours.

Create your private agenda and follow it.

Imagine your reality and hustle it.

Develop your discipline and adapt to it.

Nothing is impossible, and everything is within your reach.

CHAPTER 2

You Are Beautiful

Before I continue talking about my life, I want you the reader to realize what is happening right now: at this exact time of day, month, year, this exact moment, only one person has your name, your looks, your scent, your experience, your voice, and that one person is *you*. No other being like you exists around the world; no other person has the exact same traits as you. I learned this the hard way and went through a paralysis of feelings to realize how unique I am, and more importantly, how unique we all are, as human beings. This is why I can boldly state, "As you are, you are beautiful."

You are unique in every way possible. It is important to remember that.

Most times people get into relationships for the wrong reasons, reasons that can be innocent at first, but deadly in the long run. I will speak about my poisonous relationship in the next chapter; however, I was in a relationship that unwittingly became the idea for this chapter. The woman I was with attempted to change the being that I am, and subliminally, I accepted this. Prior to that relationship, I had not given myself the time to discover who I am and what I do/do not like, not even my smallest of hobbies. This change of my character came very close to my near destruction, and I was blind to what I was allowing myself to do.

Always remember that you will only allow certain vibes into your life, and that you need to choose carefully who you open that door to. This is why I say it was my fault I allowed her to change me, because I wanted a better "me" for her, not realizing I was already the better version of myself. As I was, I was beautiful. I did not need to change one factor or trait, not because I was perfect—I was not—but because I was simply **me**, a one-of-a-kind human being that God created. I had so many different traits and characteristics that can never, ever be duplicated; and that's what you are. You are a human being with traits, characteristics, personality, and experiences that can never be duplicated, as you are made once and that's it.

After my split out of my relationship in 2015, I immediately began working on myself and trying to figure out who I am and what I'm about, not knowing that what I was searching for was staring right back at me in my own reflection. Relationships are like society in a way; you can either be part of that society and accept it or defy that specific lifestyle and attempt to change it. Those changes aren't easy, and in most cases, they fail, and the individual comes back to who they truly were. That is not to say people can't become better versions of themselves. People can become the better versions of themselves once they let go of certain traits that impact them negatively; however, that is only up to the person to do. You cannot change an individual who does not want to change.

I had a friend read this; he indicated he read a lot of pain.

But isn't pain beauty? Take into consideration some of the most inspiring stories of the century; they all inspire through pain. It does not need to stem from major life tragedies or situations that have nearly destroyed you. You can define it in any way that you want, and that's what makes your pain beautiful. You need to understand that things aren't necessarily happening for reasons that are unexplainable and are the actions of a greater being. No. The events happening now are simply situations that are shaping you for who you need to be tomorrow. As you are now, you are beautiful, and as you will be tomorrow, you will be beautiful as well. You really do not need to know why you are going through a rough patch, why that rough patch is making you go through the pain. What you need to do is believe that you'll be able to tell stories one day about what you went through to come out on the other side.

Take the smallest of examples. A small delay in your route can have you run into a friend unexpectedly; if that delay had not occurred you would not have seen them. A small delay in your trip could be the reason you do not fall into disaster or rather be the cause of a sticky situation. If you must, debunk the myth that everything happens for a reason, and that there's a higher being working some magic, and consider what I just said. Now if you believe in that, follow what you believe in, because as you are, you are beautiful. You must believe that these present bumps and bruises will essentially make up who you are.

Stories are fun when the excitement is there. You must allow your story to be defined as your destiny chooses it to be. Regardless of the trauma that comes along with the journey, you must allow these instances to be part of your story. Do not be scared of pushing people out of your life because of your story either. Those who are willing to hear and open their heart to you are the ones who are worth the content of your life. Although at times we may feel that understanding our journey should only be possible for those who are close to us, know that it is perfectly fine to open up to the world. God knows, the world requires your beauty.

Being self-conscious about your body, weight, looks, personality, and societal perception is normal, but ask yourself, was there a standard of what you need to be and conform to when you were born? Was that not when you were most vulnerable? You were forced into this life, literally, but you were not forced to become what life asked of you. That beautiful day that you were born, you were beautiful, and as you are now, you are beautiful. As time goes by, however, you will grow and learn that you will be what you are to be regardless of the trials and tribulations. We listen, observe, and allow words from the outside world to sometimes penetrate our mind.

When we were first brought into this world, we were delivered with happiness and words of congratulations around us. As we grew older, we realized the words changed. It is important to always realize that you have the ability to shell these words out and continue on the beautiful journey you had started. Your boundaries are there, and people will judge. You may not always have the thick skin for it but know that the words thrown at you are not a reflection of yourself. Beautiful people know beautiful people. Read that again. When beautiful people want to judge other people, they will allow themselves the privilege of getting to know them. They will ask questions. They will dig deeper into who you are before using words that only reflect the image that they see.

Who are you? What are you? What do you like? Why do you not like certain things? Have you figured out what you like and don't like? All these are questions that are almost always sidestepped because we are so busy living for others that we forget that we ourselves need to live. We are much too busy seeking beauty in others and finding happiness in others that we forget it's right where we haven't looked, that is, in ourselves. You are your own ray of hope, your own umbrella of shelter, your own sunshine to your morning, and the only thing stopping you from realizing that is you.

You, as you are today, are beautiful. With your flaws and with your strengths you are built as an entity like no other. Giving time to build on yourself and to realize all the questions that a random stranger may ask you is an absolutely beautiful journey. The simplest of questions can be asked, and you may find yourself in a situation you had never considered. I want you to know that it is fine; it's okay to not know or to be lost at a certain stage in your life. Even if you haven't figured out all your moves and are stressing, that uncertainty, right now, in that stage, is perfectly fine.

You may experience this stage of life by yourself or with someone who is willing to take this journey with you. If you have that support, you are blessed beyond measure. Please know that not all of us are lucky enough to have loved ones who are willing to be patient while we find ourselves. The truth is, if you do, that individual that is supporting you is looking at something much deeper than the beauty you may see in yourself. They are looking at the understanding of your being.

Investments are only truly understood when explained, and it takes the right individual to really fathom the income and the outcome it brings. Mind you, as the reader, I do not want you to do nothing and think that is fine. No. Rather, I want you to feel comfortable where you are, and know that if you work hard and place a vision in front of you, you will attain what you want. We spend most of our time stressing about our next step and the public image that we project, so that we forget to enjoy the step we are currently walking and the reflection we see in the mirror.

When was the last time you lived for you?

Being comfortable in your own skin is a very hard task, and it is not to be taken lightly. If you are able to do it, I commend you and applaud you on achieving a level of confidence not all have. If you are the type to have panic attacks, anxiety, be overly talkative, or have very emotional traits, who is to say that is unacceptable? Some may avoid it in an attempt to keep the peace in their world, but that may be because their peace is so fragile.

In a world where change is not accommodated, why would you want to change who you are? The truth is that those who are meant to be in your life will selflessly be in your life without you asking for their presence. They will provide you with the safety and reassurance of their own free will. The ability to offer you decisiveness regarding your relationship will be on the top of their priority list.

Your actions as a human being should be acceptable to yourself by yourself first. Your presence in this life is so paramount that you might not notice your true mark until it is too late; but why wait till it's too late? Imagine this: approximately 7.9 billion people currently live in this world, and only **one** person is **you**. Why would you want to change something so unique that it can't ever be replicated? On both physical and soulful levels, it is hard to do. Mind you, you can work to become a better human, but again, you need to do that for yourself. **I repeat** that you do not need to become a better human being for anyone other than yourself.

Of course, you can have another human being become your catalyst for change, but you must remember that the change is **you**. Overly hyper? That's fine; you are who you are, and those who need to accept you will. You must not worry about others' acceptance and what this world wants you to be. Take into consideration the biggest of pop stars that ranged from the 1940s to the current day; they are all so different and unique in their own ways that they did not conform to what society asked of them; rather they polished their hidden talents and unique abilities as humans, and the world loved it.

Shine like the biggest pop star within your circle of life.

Coming from an environment and culture where I need to be careful, so that I am not judged in the wrong way and people do not speak ill of me, I had to always second-guess my every move. I had to always think about my actions and how they would be portrayed in the society or circle of people that surrounded me. In essence I thought I was doing the 'right thing,' but it was to my surprise that I ended up losing myself. I forgot how to live, how to speak my truest self in public, how to communicate my feelings, and how to be open with people. In all honesty, I was too scared to speak with individuals about my feelings, because I was not sure how they would judge me, and although I am over that now as I write this book, I still find myself doing it at times.

Even though it is a different type of trait, I still believe that I am fine as I am, and that I am as beautiful as I am going to get at this point in time. At one point, after getting out of a very toxic relationship, I realized that I needed to dedicate time to myself so that I can learn about myself and find my inner beauty. Days and months passed by without me noticing any improvements, until I had come out of my comfort zone and met a few new individuals I started a conversation with, and through our talks, I realized that I have begun my process of self-healing into my truest of being. I was asked random questions and offered certain drinks. I refused because I disliked the taste or the color. Prior to this I would accept and be in a translucent state of conforming to what's around me at any given time. I was happy; I still am and will forever be, as long as I am my truest of self. Those who need to see your beauty, or anyone else's will give the time you deserve to get to know the inner you and all that you are.

As you are right now, you are b-e-a-u-t-i-f-u-l.

Maybe you know this information and are reading because you are intrigued by the material I have offered about my life within the readings so far, but at least you are reading. I hope I can give you an insight as to what has worked for me and others around me so that you yourself can be your truest of beings. The truth is my life has had its run-ins with all types of problems, issues, happy times, etc., but that has placed me in a position where I am at an advantage. Your past is absolutely beautiful. I want you to look at your reflection right now, stare at yourself for 10 minutes, and then continue reading this section. No, really, go stare at yourself and think about all the marks on your face, your eyebrows, your lips, your eyes, your cheeks, and everything else associated with what you see. Stare and come back.

Did you by any chance see cheeks that held the tears of your past? Did you see the lips that tasted the salt as you cried for hours on end? Did you see the lips that have been kissed before (possibly by the wrong sort, who did not appreciate your every touch)? Or did you see the smile that somehow, someway made its way through all the garbage that you had been through to get to where you are now?

Your past is beautiful, and it's as beautiful as you are now. You are perfectly built to be who you are right now. An affectionate past is one to be indulged in. A human who has truly been through a lot in their past has not only developed stories to tell but created many different traits that not all people have. Take the worst situation from your past and think of how life could have panned out if you hadn't gone through it. You may have not been as strong as you are now or developed the different traits of beauty that you currently possess. Those around you who see and deal with you on a daily basis may have not been the same if you had not gone through your adversity. This goes for others, too, as you are affected by the circle of the people you surround yourself with. Your past affects your present, and your present depicts your future, and if you truly believe in your beauty now, your future is nothing short of a Picasso.

Be judged and allow those around you, whether they are your friends or foes, to judge your beauty. The fact is they cannot come to terms with their own visage, so they try to mock or speak to you about yours. Your beauty is yours to do with as you please, and if you choose to share it with the world, then good on you. The moral of this all is to be comfortable with who you are, doing what you do, and loving who you are. As you are, you are beautiful, and there isn't a soul on earth who can change that. Why would you want to change that or have someone come into your life and change who you are or what possesses you to do what you do? To be who you are, you have to be your own being and become one with that beauty.

If one day you went for a walk and you noticed a very pretty rose on the side of the path, would you pick that one rose you singled out from the rest? The fact of the matter is that it doesn't matter whether or not you pick it, but that you noticed something so unique in that one rose that you didn't about the others. If plants had feelings, would they communicate the disbelief that one isn't like the others? What did that one rose have that the others didn't? You may not know why, but you, the beholder, realized the beauty in that one rose that blossomed from a seed into what you noticed. *Life is very similar to this rose.* You were born into a world that gave you nothing but one or two (if you're lucky) loving individuals who decided to nurture you into the human you are today. Whether you are a child or an adult, you have blossomed into what you are today because of the people who took care of you, and more importantly, because of yourself. The rose did not grow on its own; it had soil, water, sun, and care. For someone to take care of it, water it, feel for it, make sure it is growing in the right environment, the rose itself would attempt to grow, and those that do are the ones that are so unique.

Rain or shine, stormy or mild weather, that rose will grow, and if damaged, it leaves seeds back behind so that the following season it grows again with what it has left behind from its past. Rather than speaking of how much you have to grow in the next couple of years, take a step back and realize how much of your past you have in you to help you with the steps you are currently taking. As you realize this, you are beautiful. If you are currently coming out of a situation that has destroyed you, and you are not capable of functioning like you used to, I am here to tell you: **it is not the end of the world**. You are a beautiful human being, a rose that has blossomed, and somehow the storm chose to wash over you. Be assured that the storm will pass, and the seeds of your current tribulations will be planted for some time in the future, where the right soil will grow this seed, and you will once again become a living rose within the sunshine. As you are, you are beautiful.

Looking inside the box rather than outside the box helps you determine what you are and why you are who you are. Determining your past and realizing what you have become in the present places you at ease. I touch base a lot on the trials of our past, as I am a very firm believer that your past will shape your present; your heart shapes your present, and your present is a clear indication of your future. We are all walking stories with beautiful beginnings, and at our core, we are deeper than words.

We are always taught at a young age to look outside the box when struggling to figure out a solution to a problem, but is that the most logical way to solve your own personal issue? After the passing of my brother, I attempted to look outside the box a lot in an effort to find a way to get better. At the time, I had experienced horror and events that depicted evil. This altered my mentality and had me looking at the world in a very ugly way. I lost my brother, my best friend, my right hand. I had started searching for a healthy relationship within myself. It wasn't until years later that it hit me: I was searching in all the wrong places. My solution was staring at me right there, in the mirror that was reflecting a destroyed individual, an individual who, at that time, did not know his place and where he belonged. All I knew was that I was going to figure it out. I started looking at more core values that I had been taught and that I had taught myself, in an effort to always keep them in mind. I realized that I had begun my healing process, and my inner beauty was now making its way out.

I find myself in situations where my friends or people that I know try giving me advice about certain things that make me who I am. If you were to ask me a few years ago, or rather prior to the accident, I would take what they were telling me seriously and change to accommodate their basic needs. Now things are different; I am who I am, and I won't change my core demeanor for anyone.

Take in what I am explaining to you as if it were you getting this advice from the friends who surrounded you. We all have those friends and family members who ask for certain changes because we do not meet their standards. This is entirely not true. It is not that you do not meet their standards; it's rather that they do not take the time to understand you and what makes you who you are. Those who truly do not question or understand why you are who you are today shouldn't be in your life.

In the next few chapters I speak about negative vibes and cutting out any poison so that you can live a more fulfilling life. You are who you are, and the past that has built you to be who you are now should allow you power over making decisions such as picking and choosing who you want in your life. I personally have stopped people from being in my life as they have never understood me and what has made me the being presented to the world. I have had people as close as family members, or people I have called family, simply state that I am "being weak" when it came to my breakdowns over the passing of my brother or my split with my ex. They never questioned why I am who I am now and never decided to view the beauty in my pain but rather judged me based on what they do not understand. They gave advice, and evidently, I still thought differently. I did what I wanted to do to heal myself, and in return I became better. I also applied this way of thinking towards others that are dealing with their own situations, to help me understand them better.

What I'm trying to say is that we all have stories of suffering, laughter, happiness, and heartbreak that we don't allow ourselves to forget. You must not ever judge someone based on how they act, as their road to that day may have been an uphill struggle that you may never view. As they are, they are beautiful, and as you are, you are beautiful. The true measure of beauty is not how beauty may make you feel but how beautiful you feel about yourself.

Exit Thoughts

It took me a while to get to the conclusions in this chapter. I have gone through many physical forms, many mental forms, and many spiritual forms to learn what beauty is.

Look, I have flaws, and I am not perfect. I've got way too much baggage. I got problems that are piled to the ceiling, issues, but ... this is who I am. I have realized we are all the same. We all have a story, and we are all fighting battles.

I can't be mad at the world for not being exactly what I want it to be. I'm going to embrace my flaws and perfections to the point where its transparent.

I get it. My past has made me who I am today. My pain from the past that is now gone exists in scars. Now imagine my life with no scars, no stories to tell, no content that could explain who I am. I'd be boring.

So ...

Be beautiful, be as you are; be YOU!

And ignore rest of the world that thinks you're anything other than that.

CHAPTER 3

Positive Vibes

Ever wonder why sometimes you find yourself stuck in a funk, in a bad mood, or simply not 100%? Take a quick look at what you're surrounded by. Forget the speeches, the misfits, the propaganda, and the people you have around you, and focus on what kind of energy you are receiving. Chances are that you're on the receiving end of a rope in a tug of war that's pulling you into a pool of negative vibes. Energy speaks volumes, and to have the right energy around you is what is truly needed in this turnpike of a life we live. It's a very simple equation, to be honest with you; however, it isn't always easy to execute and keep a positive outlook on life. Negativity can create negativity and put you into a hole of depression and stress.

40

Ever hear of the saying, "You are a product of your society?" Well, imagine you are constantly placing yourself around situations and people that spew nothing but negativity, who bring no value to your life. What do you think would happen to you? You would slowly and subliminally become a negative individual with no positive energy and then spread that negativity to other people. You won't notice it at first, until you meet someone new and realize that they don't want to be around you, or when you reflect and begin to feel it yourself.

We all face situations where we are involuntarily placed in a negative environment or mentality. Eventually, what results from these situations is feelings of depression, stress, suicidal thoughts, being upset, angry, and the list goes on. I can tell you that I was personally subject to such emotions after the loss of my brother. It came on me like a force that I had no control of; I was not accustomed to the process of healing that was required, but I was beginning to be introduced to it. In our daily lives, we begin to open ourselves up to certain vibes around us, and at times, those who spew the worst of vibes may need you to bring give them some of your positive energy.

To manifest your vibe, you must start with shelling out the negative.

Manifesting your ideas into reality and creating an image of who you are, to what you want to be, will make you become that person. Now, I don't mean that you can manifest the idea of becoming a millionaire and wake up the second day with your bank account on a roll. What I mean is that if you start with the smallest of steps into manifesting a positive emotion, you will slowly but surely realize that it all follows.

For example, take a small little emotion that you find to be a negative area and try to manifest it by seeing the positive side of it. That is all that it takes to slowly start shifting your mentality. This is definitely not "think of your goal and you will attract it;" rather this is "place yourself in an environment where you know you will attract vibes that will enhance you into becoming the supreme person you want to be." You must take time for yourself, learn to love yourself enough to be able to manifest what you want in your life. I touch on the subject of "loving yourself before you can love anyone else" frequently within these chapters, as I believe it is fundamental to becoming 100% of your untapped ability.

This is why it is important to manifest your love to yourself first. Your own being must be the vibe you are willing to walk around with and showcase to the world. You must realize that you can never look for happiness or love anywhere other than within yourself first. Too many people manifest their love and happiness in others and tend to forget to manifest it within themselves. Getting along with yourself, your truest of being, your most genuine side, and manifesting that into reality is truly an amazing feeling.

Removing the negative has many different parts and stages that one can interpret in their own way. You must start with yourself and rebuild who you are into who you want to be; you must embrace your flaws and manifest them into the beauty you want them to be. You must realize that your current flaws are beauty, your past flaws are cool, and that your future flaws will simply be epic. These flaws are what make you who you are, and, in order to embrace this manifestation of one's truest self, you must be in love with yourself.

Must you really care about anything other than what you want? No. If you are focusing on being happy, must you care about the negativity coming your way? No. Unfortunately, you will receive it, and it will be out of your hands as sometimes with the right amount of pressure even the hardest of diamonds crack. To remain in a positive state of mind is not what you should do, but instead, come to terms with what's around you and what isn't. The mistake that we all make is that we force ourselves to be positive, neglecting the facts causing us to lie to ourselves. In order to embrace your inner positive being and to create an aura of positivity, you must embrace the fact that there are negative situations around you.

A quick little story about manifesting the vibe you want to have and keeping it around you: around my birthday, I met this woman and a brief conversation with her; that was it. I didn't even get her name at that time, as I was just happy to be around friends and family. As time went by, we somehow connected and got together for the Super Bowl. I was hesitant as I usually talk to someone before heading out, a precaution based on negativity that I take to make sure they're not full of it. I went out nonetheless, and we had food, drinks, and good conversation. The waitress asked if we wanted to include our names in a ballot for a prize. Simply, she looked me dead in the eyes and said, "Go for it. If you manifest it, it will happen."

Me being me, at the time I did not understand this. I never win these things. However, I placed my name and sat back. Ten minutes later during halftime, they announced the winner. I had won, and I kind of lost my breath for a second out of sheer excitement. One thing this person didn't know was that, as I was walking back from claiming my prize, I realized how much she had changed my life with the simple words, "Just believe, manifest it, and it will happen." I sat back down, looked over, and she uttered, "The universe works in mysterious ways."

We are all impacted by those around us, and we meet the people we meet for special reasons. One cannot live a lifetime without those around them. This is why it is so important to make sure the circle of people around you are those you can be 100% comfortable with.

Show me who your friends are, and I'll tell you who you are.

I never really understood what it meant when my mother would say that to me, until I realized that the individuals around me were not who I wanted them to be.

I became them.

I became the same people they were, the gossiper, the drama-setter, the one with the negative outlook on life, the one who cared about things that did not matter, and the one who always saw the cup as half empty. Taking a step back, I began to realize I was hustling for acceptance rather than for my own happiness. (That acceptance I speak of in the next few chapters delayed the process of me being at peace with myself.) Forgetting the main principle of "hustle 4 happiness" insanely messed me up. My vibe was an utter disaster, and I began to realize that when I was no longer around that group of people but was alone. My actions would totally imitate them; meanwhile they were nowhere to be found.

Catching your reflection in the mirror as totally worn out and beat constitutes a change of lifestyle. Don't be fooled by what you see though. We all have stories, and some people who may be viewed as positive are actually going through their own problems and challenges. I have heard that exact saying from a lot of people, but it is one thing to hear it and another to see it. Positivity isn't just a trait you put out to people, words that are said, or an image that is portrayed just for people to see. Rather it is a vibration you put out that is felt by yourself and others. True embodiment of positive traits can only be nurtured if your mind is in total acceptance of your surroundings. This acceptance of your surroundings will allow you to find and to view all of life's bluffs, flaws, and beauty. One must be able to have others feel their positivity without acting or uttering a word. I have been around people who look like they are on top of the world, at a new level of positivity, and then, within 2 seconds, you can tell there is a huge façade being portrayed.

When the sun is set, you really need to come to the realization yourself of where you currently are in life. Are you a negative human? Is it your circle that's causing you to be this way? What is not aiding your thinking process of change? What do you currently want from your life? Can you or should you change the negative in your life to help make you better?

These questions of self-realization are not a negative thing. Think about it: if you sit there and realize that you're one human creature that is stuck within a dome of situations that are neither positive nor helpful, you're already on your way up. This process is never negative. It can't be. There's absolutely no way.

Do you think that two negatives don't make a positive? Wrong. If you're living a negativity-filled life and coming to the realization that you are a negative creature, you're already in the positive. I label it "creature" and not "human being" for a reason. We as humans are placed on this earth to live and eventually be given back to earth as used capsules. Our soul, thoughts, and aura are only here for a limited time within this capsule we call our body.

So, what are you going to do with that body while you are here in tangible form? Will you do good unto others? Will you treat yourself fairly? Will you allow yourself the positive bubble and circle of people you deserve to have in your life, or will you bend as the shade of negativity overcomes your actual being? Being positive wasn't always this easy for me, truly. I'd be the biggest liar if I told you that it was that simple. To this very day, I have times of hardship where I find myself searching for an ounce of positivity.

I ended up getting out of my comfort zone during the last quarter of 2018. I stopped going to the clubs and partying, as I had a feeling that kind of lifestyle was imposing on my endurance while seeking a positive life. When I took that step back, I was able to see the world on a much larger scale. This step back enabled me to realize the validity of my thinking and what was causing it. I loved my crew and the individuals I went out with, but I realized at one point that it wasn't they who were the source of the poison of negativity within my life, rather it was the atmosphere. I found myself in situations I have never encountered and were counter-intuitive for my future. I saw no content and no context within that nightlife followed by lazy Saturdays and Sundays dealing with major hangovers. Finding out that it was my own doing that took me away from the positive-vibe lifestyle I had built, I knew I had to build it back up once again.

You may have found yourself in that type of atmosphere as well at some point of your life. You may have wanted out as well, as you probably thought it didn't serve your life. That type of thought process is fine, and you are beautiful with the way you think. The atmosphere creates a fun-filled time, but what happens after hours? After the loud music is dead and the crowds have dispersed home? At times the only positive vibe is the party itself, as it takes us away from the reality that we face. This type of cover-up was never healthy and was never a long-term fix. We found love and happiness in the moment, and if we were lucky enough, we walked away with much more than that.

When I stepped away, I realized that the friends I partied with continued their lives unaffected in the same route they always had. Some till this day are still dancing to that loud music. Some have started strong, financially independent, long-term businesses that have left such a positive effect on people. You must be positive to cut the poison. Stagnancy will absolutely kill you and so will comfort. When I stepped away, I focused on achieving the results I had longed for, and even though they took 2 years, I was finally where I needed to be. You won't see immediate results, rather it will take you a while to see the change you wish for and require.

While writing this book, I found positivity in areas of my heart that I thought were blacked out. I had gone through ... let's call it an "end of an experience" with someone that I considered a potential partner. I tried to look at every possible part of our past as negative, but I couldn't. I wasn't sure why it was the way it was; however, I realized one thing: it was my perspective. I realized that I could be negative or rather embody negative thoughts. I don't believe anyone is truly a "negative" human, rather they are embodied by temporary negative thoughts. We sometimes are a product of our environment, but only to the extent we allow ourselves to be. We need these negative vibes, so that we can recognize the positive out there and appreciate it when we reach that level.

You as a human being can hold in so much life and happiness rather than pain and resentment. It is hard at times to choose the happiness in life, but it's a must to survive and accomplish anything worthwhile. I have learnt the "forgive and let go with no apology method." This has allowed me to seriously forgo my negative thoughts and somehow embody the true realization of peace. It's what we all chase at the end of the day, isn't it?

It's a yin and yang type of thing.

Back to what I was saying, I could have been very negative; however, I began looking at things in a different light. I didn't want to continuously condemn the good times or rather give in to the bad thoughts that entered my mind, which would have essentially affected my body and soul. Within the two-week period of our split, I realized that I was exhausted and didn't want to always wake up feeling tired because of my anger and negativity. I had a talk with the person who gave me the best advice and the only person I trusted: my reflection.

I had said to myself that I needed to go to the basics and look at the cup as half full rather than half empty. Instead of looking at my situation that didn't work out, I started looking at it as an experience that allowed me to feel some type of love, to be happy and experience feelings I thought were dead, the beginning of a new chapter. Who knew how it was supposed to go? I was blessed to be able to realize my heart had room to love again, and for those 2 years, I was able to love beyond my capable mind. My heart was still in ruins. I had just lost my best friend, my girlfriend, and my partner in crime. However, I had myself left, and that was all I ever needed.

You see, all my life I have been backed into a corner, fending and fighting off evil and negativity, on my way to success. It didn't seem right for me to give up now and allow this to destroy me. I forgave her without an apology or telling her I forgave her, and that it wasn't for her, but rather *for me*. I was subconsciously forgiving myself and getting out of the negative state of mind. Within a week, I was able to wake up with energy and become productive again. I didn't need to be in a negative state of mind anymore.

If you are ever encased in a situation that has you in a blanket of curiosity regarding closure with your ex-partner, GET DISTRACTED! Stay busy and force yourself out of your thoughts; the closure you think you need will do you no good. The ability to learn things that no longer serve you is useless and will give no substance to your life. Are you wondering why you really didn't get the job? What does that do you for you? Are you wondering what your ex-partner is now thinking of you, or rather the relationship, and their reflections? Who cares? What are they doing? Chances are they're not even worried about what you're dealing with, so why should you? Not sounding selfish or egotistical, but you really are weighing yourself down for someone who is sailing across the seas in breezy winds. I know it is tough and it is not easy, but life is difficult.

We come across so many emotions and feelings throughout the day that sometimes we really get overwhelmed. Let your emotions speak out, let your anxiety seep through; however, keep your pride and dignity intact. What once served you no longer does. What once cared for you no longer does. What once held Titanic-type love no longer floats for you. Do you believe that it is healthy or beneficial for you to find and search for the reason things fell apart? I used to. I really did. I thought at times that it would be good and helpful so that I can overcome the situation. Turns out it was all a scam.

We really do not need closure or justification. Here's why: people have their opinions about others no matter what. Truth is, you have a different mental profile in each person's mind. Some will say you are resilient and powerful while others say you are weak and gullible. The next person may speak of an amazing story that involves you while the other will speak on such tragic events. These opinions are totally subjective, which is why it is so important to create that positive confidence in yourself. Know yourself. Know the story that embodies you and always be aware of those who may be going through their own situations. This not only allows you to protect your bubble of positivity, but rather to keep your aura safe enough to reflect your personality and life.

What I'm saying is this: sometimes you are your own anchor, stuck on something that isn't serving you, in an ocean of negativity. You have to learn to either pull that anchor out or drop it in some positive waves. You can be your worst enemy. Sometimes the anchor is what is holding you back. Assess your situation, think about what it is that is anchoring you. If you find the cause of the problem, cut that anchor, and **let it go.**

If the wind blows west, sail west.

Do not think that being positive all the time is a good thing. Allowing yourself to realize that it's okay to not be positive is the main goal here. A 'POSITIVE VIBES ONLY' mentality is nonsense and is an extremely destructive mentality. You have to allow yourself to realize what isn't positive and what you can do about it to change. If you are faced with a situation that does not give you or itself a positive nuance, break it down and figure out what is needed for you to beat the opposition. There is no such thing as always remaining positive. You will have your ups and downs, which will cause you to realize you are really in control of it all.

Now to get a little more personal.

Down in the gutter, feeling more depressed than I have ever been during the COVID-19 pandemic, has taught me a few things. Even those closest to you will not sacrifice their peace to bring you back to life. Take it for what it is; I did. I suffered from my depression and anxiety to a level of no return at one point during the ill-forsaken pandemic. When my anxiety and depression was at an all-time high, and I had just finished my court case, 2 days before my brother's birthday, my relationship fell apart. It was devastating. I found myself in such a negative place where I couldn't handle life anymore and became suicidal.

Why? It was simple. It was compound emotional interest.

It was a state of emotional debt that I had dug myself into involuntarily. I realized that I had been through some hard times and that the person I was with didn't make it easier. Now can I blame the person I am with? Yes, of course I can. (The timing was off but that is beside the point.) That weekend, a part of me died, again. I remember waking up on my brother's birthday and realizing that we had finally finished convicting the last of the individuals that caused us pain, and I still didn't have my brother, that I didn't have the one person I thought I could lean on. I was taken from this world at an early stage and thrown into a pool of negative, bloodthirsty individuals who sucked the life out of me.

But 2 days later I woke up and realized something. I was heartbroken over someone who had it in them to walk away from me when I was at my lowest, and nothing I could say or do would bring my brother back. We all know the phrase "the only way out is up," and that was exactly what I did. I stepped out, I stepped up, I chose me, and I chose to become okay without anyone's help, and that is exactly what I did. What else could I do? What else was there a possibility for me to do? I had to **choose** to be positive. I was backed into a corner with the world coming at me from all angles and at one point I had contemplated death. I wasn't a coward, though, and although that would've allowed me to see my brother sooner, I didn't want to see him like that or have my parents ache in the pain of losing both their sons.

I realized the catalyst to my depression was someone who chose to leave for their reasons. Although the motive this person had was pure and unintentional, it only served them. Some of us are fighting our own negativity and battles that we do not know how to deal with under pressure. You can be sleeping with someone, loving someone, and still not touch an inch of their soul. I wasn't able to understand why or what happened to cause this, but I knew the purity of this person's heart. I was hurt in the beginning, but I couldn't look at the situation in a negative light. I forgave her and communicated the thoughts behind what happened, only to find out that this person was fighting their own battles as well. You must be considerate to the unknown. I was fighting my own battles, yes, and as strong as I may have been, my forever love was dealing with her battles too. After a little time apart, we were able to communicate the issues that eventually brought us back together and helped us relearn communication. I was angry before I became content and positive.

How could I allow this temporary feeling to dictate my life? I certainly wasn't going to go back to taking meds to numb the pain again, so I chose what every capable man is of doing, and I resorted to something that makes me happy. I chose one thing that I knew would make me happy regardless of what state of mind I was in and that was my motorcycle. I was able to go for a long ride and clear my mind and focus on one pain at a time.

You have to take yourself out of your situation. You have to find a positive item, thing, or activity that makes you happy and chose it 100 times over. The ability to overcome the smallest negativity is the largest and most powerful trait you as a human being have. Maybe you'll have someone to help you, or maybe your circle of friends or support system is much more supportive than mine was at the time, and if so, *you are blessed*.

Use whatever means necessary to get out of your bubble and get back to the normal you. If you are feeling that you need someone to talk to, go see a therapist or talk to your mom. Your significant other should not be your go-to when it comes to shelling out these negative thoughts. It burdens them and really can place a strain on the relationship, and believe me, I learnt the hard way. You are surrounded by a support system that allows you to get different opinions on what you are going through, and it is so important that you protect your relationship aura. Your partner is there for you and should be there for you through it all, but as a man, if you need the help, seek it. There is no shame in seeking a more positive lifestyle that can essentially help you change the trajectory of your personal life.

If you are feeling anxious or depressed, try seeing a therapist or speaking to a very close friend. This negative feeling can change and talking to someone can help your personal or relationship life as well. I am not saying that you shouldn't speak to your partner about what bothers you but rather be selective, as your partner may be fighting so many battles as well that they don't come to you about. You see, if you are looking for a best friend in a partner, that is great, that's what makes things work. However, at times, best friends have to look out for each other, and spewing negativity into their life isn't the most positive thing you can do.

Feeling negative isn't negative, it's a feeling. This feeling makes you human, it makes you alive. Feel it, feel every inch of it, and then turn it into what you need it to be to fuel the fire within you. It is your time to embody a soul of positivity, a heart that belongs to that soul and a mind that is in line with your soul and heart. Adapt to your vibes, size them up, and learn how to sell the idea of who you were before this rush of negativity took place. Sell yourself to the you that you want to be, to the more positive you, to the you who knew life is beautiful and worth living. Walk barefoot, get grounded, stop, and take in the scenery … and then keep on moving to your goals and your future.

Man or woman, never sell yourself short of the experience of life. Understand that the positive outcome can only be generated if the negativity has been realized. If you see that the life you have with a friend or a partner is worth the sacrifice, help that individual get through the pain by directing them to solutions. We can only become positive and embody a vibe the moment we execute on the process of admitting the negativity behind our actions and thoughts. Relax your mind, ease your soul into peace, and allow your heart to beat normally again; it'll all be alright. You are not a negative person but rather a person who is going through a negative situation. Situations change and so do thoughts ... Step back, think about what is needed and execute.

That is what worked for me, and maybe it will for you too.

Exit Thoughts

These chapters encompass so much of my livelihood that I sometimes get lost in my train of thought. I want to write, yet I find myself only communicating to you what my heart truly feels when it comes to the subjects that I am writing about.

Positivity has been such a key aspect of my life. I have lost friends because I have dipped into the negative field and then gained so much more. I truly had no hate in my heart during these periods and still don't; however, I have grown so fond of what I can do as a human being to get out of that negative space. I believe you can as well.

I am no different than the next person reading this or the person sitting next to you. I want you to truly understand that, because it is important that we are on the same page. Some pain I won't get over, and I will forever have that little bit of negativity overshadowing me. But now I know I can get out of it. I can't tell you what to do but rather show you how I got out of my funk, and maybe you can relate.

The point of this all is for you to relate and for me to get this weight off my shoulders. I want you to get that weight off yours as well. Whether it is to forgive and forget or get yourself into that positive state of mind, you must do better for yourself and the legacy you are willing to leave behind. I leave you mine.

CHAPTER 4

Risk

I t's scary, no doubt. The fact of the matter is that we take risks in everything that we do on a daily basis. Whether it's getting out of bed and getting ready for work or quitting your job to pursue that which makes you happy. Jumping right into what risk is and how to apply it is not what I plan on doing here. I want to explore the risks that were presented to me, and in that way, maybe you can relate.

Truly every chapter in this book is inspired from events or individuals in my life. Some may still be around, and some are unfortunately not. However the risk that was taken with each of them is not one I regret. The risk that was presented in every situation was never really brought to surface; rather it was hidden and only shown at the climax of the situation. The initial thought that would pop into my head would be when emotions (the 'sixth sense') got involved. That thought was not risk but rather just enjoying the moment. This was followed by the development of emotion after my other 5 senses were already involved. The risk is then presented with an incentive that is as simple as a word that is uttered or a feeling that is felt. This is when the risk is realized and shown.

I was offered a risk towards the beginning of 2018. This risk was someone that I had met; and it wasn't shown to me until I felt this gut feeling in my stomach and my heartbeat sped up. It was a specific situation that I was around, but even more of an experience that I had to go through with the person. This situation was different; it had me walking in awe, thinking of the exact place and time I let my walls down. The risk was clear as day. Either I take a risk on this human being and give it my all, or I shy away from it and walk away.

"I am taking the risk."

In return, I could get absolutely nothing from this person and be placed in a position that I never thought I would be. However, my gut told me that the risk needed to happen. Truly the risk wasn't me taking it for myself at all; it was risking my personal life for this human. As I mention in the previous chapter, "As you are, you are beautiful." We all have flaws, and part of that risk was both our perfections and imperfections reflecting one another.

Always remember that whatever the situation, you must embrace your inner human regardless of how cutthroat the risk. As a human with flaws, I know for a fact that I am taking a risk on myself every single day, with everything I do. When presented with this specific risk, I knew that if I did not take it, I would remain in the same position I have been for the past few years. I am talking about mentally accepting someone into my life, not about status. I, just like any of you, have sheltered myself from emotion because of the walls that I have built from my previous relationships. I knew that if I took this risk on this human, it might not only show my character, my effort, my support, and my ability to care, but it would also take me out of my comfort zone. I took the reality of the hustle and hustled what I wanted into the reality I was eager to find.

But is there anything wrong with taking a risk on someone you think is worth it? I mean someone with walls, pain, their past—is that someone to risk your time and effort on? It is totally subjective, but we are human, and if there is anything I have learned through my pain, struggle, and walls that I built, it is that we all have stories that are beautiful. Cautious as you may be, it is not your job to save the human you are taking a risk on, but rather it is you showing them that they are worth sacrificing your time for their value. While the sixth sense (emotion) has kicked in, it is always important to remember to never lose yourself while you take a risk on someone. That someone with whom you are risking your being should only be offered your truest self. While taking a risk during that time, I realized that there were a lot of new things I did not know about myself. You too will realize this. This risk that you may take can be taken on anyone in your life; it is up to you to decide if the risk is worth it and how much of your being are you willing to give to them.

"Risk me first; you come next."

If you do not love yourself first, how can you love someone else? If you do not take risk on yourself first, how can you take a risk on another? I mention the walls I built previously, and being inspired by others, I learned that sometimes knocking them results in more help than damage. Again, this is totally subjective. Gauge your audience as you might before you do any of this, for only you can be the master of your destiny and fate.

In this section of the chapter, I'm going to touch on the topic "risking you first." Within our daily activities that blind us with social media and the image society wants us to project, we forget that we need to place a risk on ourselves first prior to taking a risk on another person. In essence, this means that you must learn to prioritize yourself. You must take the time off that you need, whether it is from online interactions, negative people, friends, or even family and take a risk on getting to know yourself first.

When I lost my brother, I was occupied in other people's time. I call this a parallel universe, because when you take a risk on others without gaining trust in yourself first, you're not really living in reality. I'm not saying there is anything wrong in this, but those who get into relationships to find happiness because they are not truly happy alone are individuals who have not yet risked themselves. When you really allow yourself the ability to learn, to take time away from everyone and adapt to silence, you really begin to develop. Your dislikes and your description of who you are change.

In the beginning of this chapter, you realized that you are truly a resilient human who can become a fighter in life. This is the risk that you take when that wall of separation between yourself and the person you want to become is taken down. Most of us knock down walls and move into new areas to become better human beings for other people, or rather because of other people. In most cases relationships (regardless of what or who is in them) are the catalyst for this change. We forget that the most important one of all is the relationship with ourselves. The doubt we keep within us at times kills all future ability to change. Whether it is good or bad change, we find ourselves in moments of weakness that don't really do much other than kill our lust for life.

Imagine you took a risk on that stock that was valued at $2 and valued a year later at $120. What caused you to not take that risk? Do you ever ask yourself if it is your surroundings? Or is it what you are afraid to lose?

You see, at times what we don't do, we do to our future selves. When you give into this fear of risk and do not act upon what you believe could be a great thing, you remain stagnant. Now, if you have a fear of gambling with large numbers, take calculated risks. But if this risk is dependent on interactions, you're better off not taking it. We're only human, and we have the ability to lose and to win. Whether it is approaching someone for a new business venture and pitching your idea, or calling a client for a sale, these are all types of risk you can afford to attract.

For my guys out there, if you're reluctant and don't believe you can risk introducing yourself with the attractive girl that you're crushing on, then you've already failed. For the strong, independent women out there who feel as if some jobs or situations may not be fitting for them, but who want to go for it anyways, then take the risk. Take the risk by any means necessary and weigh your outcome. The idea is to manifest your mind into the outcome you want for the risk you are willing to take. What's the worst that can happen? Rejection?

Well, at least if you get rejected you have an answer as to what you were curious about. Being rejected is directly correlated to the courage you had in taking that risk. The outcome may have not been in your favor, but you learned a lesson of what does not work. This knowledge can be specified as the income that the outcome brought to you. The beauty of this is that it can be applied to any situation that you may encounter in the future or present.

Now, if acceptance is the result, then the reward of you taking the risk is satisfactory. You feel a sense of accomplishment because you became a winner and the return on your investment is in some form of a "yes." In this case, you learn what does work, and you move on to the next risk. That mentality, the positive one that you develop when you win, is key to keeping a sense of humility. You must apply the same mentality when you lose as well.

Controlling your emotions plays a huge role for the outcome of your risk as well. Letting your walls down comes with an emotional pool of thoughts and feelings. When risk isn't taken, your wall may be erect and as strong as ever with a foundation you have set. But what good are strong walls if you do not build around them? The moment you start letting your walls down and begin to believe in your heart or what it is you are doing, then the risk becomes second nature.

Wall by wall, they all fell down.

Being vulnerable is being risky with yourself first, and there isn't anything wrong with risking your vulnerability towards society. Caught up in today's laws that govern what we should and shouldn't do, we all get lost in thoughts of acceptance of others rather than the acceptance of ourselves. Is there something wrong with that? Of course. Think about it: if Tupac Shakur did not embrace who he was and conformed to what the music industry and society wanted him to be, would he be a legend? Nope. If your idol did not stick to their guns and risk their personality for their love of self, would they have been the idol you now look up to? This could be as simple as a parent or guardian, sibling, cousin, or a family member whom you look up to. The risk that we take on ourselves first is the risk that is most important as that is the privilege given to us at birth. Here's a little personal story of mine for you to connect with, as this book is a read for you to find something that I have been through and that you can relate to.

Growing up, I was always the kid who had to take care of my little brother and was always placed in a position of responsibility. After my brother's passing, my responsibility was not gone with him; it basically just transferred to my parents. The years that followed were occupied with me forgetting myself and not risking myself at all. I was taking care of everyone and forgetting to occupy myself with my own happiness. There came a time in 2015, after I had split up from a failed engagement, that I had decided to risk the next 2 years of my life on myself. I had done some self-reflection and realized that I hadn't dedicated time to learning about myself. Although I caught a lot of resentment from my family and friends, I knew I had to spend some time on my own to get to know my surroundings. How was I supposed to risk my love again with someone else if I couldn't move to the beat of my heart?

Who am I?

I couldn't figure out the simplest of questions, and it was ridiculous. I sat and realized I couldn't even answer 21 first-date questions. What was my favorite color? What did I want in a woman? Where was I going career wise? When did I lose my self, trying to save everyone else?

All these questions, and I had no answers.

This is when I realized that I had to risk the next 2 years at minimum doing whatever I wanted to in an effort to risk my time in learning about myself. In return, not everyone was on board with my mission to recreate—or rather create—my new being. The old me was not one who was focused on what was important for self-efficacy but rather was focused on the preservation of others, yet I was not able to create a human who would reflect my original values and what I stood for. This was a destructive path that had led me to feel as if the world was moving forward while I remained stagnant.

If there was one thing I hated, it was being exactly where I was 2 years ago.

If you pay close attention, you will realize that those closest to you will do nothing but deter the idea of becoming a better human. I am talking about your immediate family or the closest friends. This could be caused by the idea that your ability to outdo your parent's productivity creates the inability to perceive success. You're basically becoming a threat, a human who is doing what they couldn't do. With the path that I chose, I realized I was becoming exactly who I wanted to be, because now I was no longer risking the fact that I was blaming others for my actions but rather pointing the finger back at myself. (The next chapter will touch on why I blame myself for all that has happened and nobody else.)

The biggest risk I took was love.

In the 2 years spent with myself I fell in love with myself. I began to realize that everything within me is what I need to be and what I want to be. The risk of heartbreak is always there, even when it's falling in love with yourself. Sometimes we become individuals that develop bad habits and the ability to become monsters, but that's just the risk we have to take.

The sixth sense is one that you need to pay close attention to as it can come out of any type of situation. While emotion allows all your other senses to be magnified and to allow you to feel utter euphoria, it could be your worst enemy. We associate emotion with everything the moment we realize that risk is involved. Whether it is base jumping or jumping into love with someone, the moment your sixth sense kicks in, you're doomed. Think about it and take away emotion from the next situation you are in, and you will begin to realize that the decision to take a risk is fairly simple.

This is you being a combination of vulnerable and risky. One must realize that the sixth sense is only as bad as you make it. The reality of the situation is that only when you look at making the sixth sense your friend will you realize the true ability to master your life. The emotion kicks in, but this state only creates a human being you never thought existed. We start doing things, saying things, expressing ideas that we never thought would exist, but the sixth sense is there to remind us that we are still human, and that we can risk being emotional. Behind closed doors, everyone embraces this sense however not everyone brings it to light. There is risk in that as well; in the world we currently live in people are not kind, but rather to live off the impulse of attacking for reasons that may be beyond us. The questions you want to ask yourself always is, "Do you want to be same as the others, or risk standing out, and being you?"

We are all created equal but different. We as beings, regardless of culture, religion, or race are created as humans, and it is then that we begin to risk the different aspects of life to become who we are. Don't think it's crazy; it's as simple as 1+1=2. It really is. Becoming the best version of you while taking the biggest risk in life is rewarding.

Getting into different situations while I was overseas after the accident allowed me to realize that not only is life "short," but it is beautiful. This beauty can be viewed in different ways, and it is up to you to look at it in the way you want to. Risk the time out of your day and look at it in an optimistic way and reflect on that. (As you can tell my thoughts are sometimes scattered; don't expect me to come up with a relevant quote for that, either.)

Throughout the times of thought and reflection there was always one thing that I found was common with all my goals and ambitions. This element was the risk of overstepping fear. For what is risk if fear is nonexistent? Aren't we always afraid of risk because of an uncertain future event? An event that may or may not occur, or better yet, an event that does not currently exist?

What if the risk that you need to take today is standing on the other side of fear? If you don't take that risk, will you know what's available for you behind the closed door that you decided to close yourself? Ignoring the risk was what got me through into my non-comfort zone. Often when I sat there wondering if I should go with a new crowd of people to an event or walk into a class of 40 people not knowing a single soul, or even change companies, I noticed that the fear was all in my head, and honestly, the end result wasn't bad at all.

The only thing I fear now is fear itself.

Have you ever taken the time to find yourself? Risked the fact that you may lose friends, family, and gain enemies? I have been going through a phase where I have not risked the time I need for personal improvement, the time I needed or need to grow as a human being, because I have been fearful of risking my friendship with people, failing to realize that those who want to be around us or who value our truest being will always understand and never allow our own personal improvement to get in the way of the relationship.

You see, I am surrounded by a lot of people who are successful, both financially and mentally. I myself am successful to a degree; however, I am still human, and throughout the trials and tribulations of life, I hit a wave of emotions that might bring down my overall demeanor.

Although we all have paths and a pre-written destiny (agree with me or not—it's up to you), mine was changed in 2011, and it's something I have accepted. I truly believe that we all have that one incident that changes us completely, that one moment, that one second, that one time where the earth falls off its axis and gravity doesn't matter. Believe it or not, that's life taking a risk on you. That is when you will be placed in the biggest test of your life, where God allows you to determine whether or not you will succeed. ***The choice is up to you***. Will you take the risk and run it for success or leave it to others who are willing to give it all up for that risk of happiness?

The previous statement may have been a little vague, so let me clear that up. I was given two choices (you are always given two choices in life when it comes to tragedies or problems). My brother's passing was no joke, and I'll talk a lot about it. But I was faced with two choices: either let the depression take over **or** risk a new way of life to help myself get out of it. Risk was also added by my father, as we had left the country and he stayed back in Toronto.

When in Lebanon, it was a new life for my mother and me. The risk was clear as mud, smacked us right in the face when it was time. I remember sitting down with my mother and asking her what she wanted out of all that, and her answer was simple: "For this not to have happened." But we all know that the passage of time is a permanent one. We cannot cry our past away, and we cannot change the now. Following that statement were tears of pain and emotions that rocked the soil under our hearts.

We spoke, and through our four-hour conversation we realized that we had to risk a new life to become strong again. The solution was that we would stay where we were and risk everything to become better again. This involved us having a new life, a new beginning, new surroundings, new family members, and a new mentality toward life. Here's the thing: nobody told us we had to go to that extent, and believe me when I tell you, every day was a new risk for us to encounter and live with.

Sometimes in life, another soul can be your strength.

There have been other situations where I've had to make a choice and risk the consequences, choices where the outcome was unknown but the path for a better life was right there in front of me. In my case, this meant risking the environment I lived in, my friends, my family, my bank account, my mentality, my culture, and the list goes on! But with every decision, if the mentality is right, a positive outcome is always the result.

With every risk taken, a reason is given to another human to be in your life. If understood correctly, you will always find support in the decisions you make and the risks you take regarding any aspect of your life. If that person is not presented to you immediately, you take that risk, and I promise you, the right individual will present themselves to support the risk that you need to take.

Life is but a journey, and the end is death.

Well, "that escalated quickly." True, but if that is not accepted at a young age, how are we to understand risk? For we are nothing but borrowed bodies with souls that last forever, on this planet for a certain amount of time. Remember that you live every day but only die once, so live your life as you want it to be.

I started this chapter by speaking about someone who inspired me to take a chance on myself and to allow me to be truly at my absolute highest level of vulnerability, and now I am speaking about the ultimate promise given to us: death. I have tied these two together, as that was a time of growth that showcased the truest vulnerability within myself. if I were to die tomorrow, I would be content, as I have shown my human being (myself) all the love I could have given at a certain time. I showed myself that I am still able to take risk on myself. As it is inevitable that we all pass away, that isn't what we risk being human beings.

What if it doesn't work out for me in the end?

You need to assess the fact that risk is taken when the moment makes most sense. An outcome may be probable; however, it cannot be predicted 100%. Now, if the risk that you took does not work out in your favor, you need to take your emotions and place them to the side. At the times these emotions are welcomed behind closed doors, we truly despise them.

You see, the risks that I took throughout the years would sometimes be in my favor, which gave me great satisfaction. I believe it would, too, for you in your situation if the odds were in your favor. I learned along the way to be as humble in my wins as I would be in my losses.

Do what you can for those who you love while you are walking on God's green earth. If that means taking a risk and going beyond the measure of what they would do for you, then do it. Your legacy is what you leave behind and that is what matters most. Take that risk, be brave, courageous, and loving for those who mean something to you, for they can be gone in a blink of an eye, and you might live with days of regret and seas of repentance.

My losses—I hate speaking about them, but in order to recognize my wins, I have to give them credit. Recognition of what didn't work out for me is praised on a higher level than my wins. My wins taught me what worked, but my losses showed me my ability to find what *can* work. I've always asked myself, "Why isn't my situation working? Is there anything I can do to fix it or help with the mindset that I am currently in?" Don't get me wrong, I don't prize my losses, but I never forget about them.

Exit Thoughts

Sometimes the risk that you take on a human being may not be the one you want, or it may not play out in your favor; however, there's something to say about a gut feeling. Trusting your gut is real regardless of the outcome of the situation. Whether it is risk towards a human being, a relationship, a career, or simply choosing a menu item, your intuition should lead you.

Life is cruel, but you have to make the best of it. Risk the time it takes you out of the day to reach out to the person who means most to you. Understand that the depth of your soul can only be understood by vulnerability. Believe that taking risk and listening to your heart could be two of your best benefactors in life. Give your vulnerability to those who are willing to dive deep into what makes you who you are. Create a connection with people who are looking to explore more than just the world with you but rather explore the world within you.

These are simply my thoughts, a way of me giving you more than just lessons. This is a page of me letting you deep into my personal life, so that we are connected on a personal level. At the end of the day, I live with no regret, and you have to learn to let go of the past mistakes regardless of the outcome. Risk is the essence of every decision.

What are you risking today?

CHAPTER 5

Man in the Mirror

I t's easy, isn't it? Wait until you get the blame put on you, without your consent. Ever have a whole crowd point their fingers at you and say, "It's your fault"? It happens every second of every minute of every day of our lives. We tend to forget that we are the first to point fingers at others without pointing a finger at ourselves.

When was the last time you secretly blamed yourself for the situation you were in? Do you ever think that others are not the reason for your failure, but rather you are? How your actions of yesterday, last year, and right now are the main reasons you are not where you want to be?

But I can't control my surroundings.

Is that for you to even control? By the way, don't be weirded out that this chapter is starting off with questions. I will constantly be asking questions to help you understand where I am coming from. A question is always best answered with a question, as it leads to a longer conversation (unless it's a cop).

Are your surroundings the ruler of all that exists in your life? Do you not like to adapt the environment you are in according to your standards? Would you not want to have certain aspects of your life changed to fit the image you mentally created for yourself? "But how can I take the blame for what my surroundings have done?" Don't you think that if you mustered up the courage you could do something about the surroundings that place a hold on you? Couldn't you find a way to change that? Would you think that it's easier using the environment and everyone else around you as the scapegoat for blame rather than yourself? Or is that too much to bear?

Yes, it's much easier and human nature to not take blame for the instances in our lives when it comes to situations that do not play out in our favor. These not-so-favorable moments are the exact moments that we need to do a reality check and say, "I'm the core of the problem, I'm the issue, I am the only one to blame." It's like when your team accomplishes something great, and you are there to either take credit or say congratulations. However, when your team (that is, LIFE) does not work in your favor, you are faced with the only choice: to take the blame. It is on you that you did not lead your team properly. This is life and its choices.

Are you the driver or the passenger?

Same thing goes for coaches: they lead their teams, notice each player's weaknesses and strengths, and then they make plays based on those skills. What's stopping you? Denial? Emotion? Forgetfulness? Stop it. Be the driver, not the passenger.

If you make a wrong turn, take the blame for it, adjust, and make the correction. Blaming yourself is the first step in forgiveness when it comes to advancing in life. I learned this the hard way over the past 7 years. Issues arose where I let my team down (my life, my family, my surroundings, and me), which led me to a long road of self-learning and soul-searching. The reason things weren't going my way was mainly because of me, truly.

Let's think about that sentence a little differently. "The reason things weren't going my way was mainly because of me, truly". How is it that uncontrollable instances are your fault, you may ask? They aren't. Unless I am creating them by the way I react to them, which is my fault. Losing my brother was an instance where I had no control over the situation. It had to happen as that was what life gave my family and me. Later reactions, though, were my fault, and I take full responsibility for the slacking, depression, stress, and the stubbornness that I caused.

You really are freed the moment you look in the mirror and realize that you have control over your life the way you've always wanted. Your reflection is your best friend, and the worst enemy negativity could have. The positivity in you exists to get you out of the rut you are in. Taking the blame for situations allows you to find peace in the problem you are facing. Blaming yourself becomes nothing but a mere metaphor for timely forgiveness. Can you take the blame for creating happiness? You will, and why?

Because it is your own doing, and you caused it.

Now do the same when things go wrong, and you need to deal with the outcome of a situation that you created or reacted to. ***Take ownership of your reactions***. That is key, forget the actions that caused you to be in the situation you are in but rather the reactions that caused you to remain in the situation you are in. You have control over that, the post-drama phase. In engineering, we call it "damage control." Control your emotions, adapt to new dynamics, forget fear, and do not overthink.

Taking the blame for your reactions is huge. I remember in 2015, after my ex and I broke up, when there was a lot of anger and resentment over the issue from my end. I was furious with the way things ended and the amount of tension that was there that stemmed from two people who "loved" each other. I hated the fact that I couldn't stand the thought of her after our break and never wanted to be around those who had a relationship remotely close to her. I remember driving and thinking to myself that I needed to forgive her for everything that she had done and for the way things played out post-breakup. It wasn't to forgive her because she had done me wrong, but rather, to forgive her so that I could move on. A part of that forgiveness was me realizing I was to blame for the reaction I took post-breakup.

I could have handled things differently, thought more logically, been able to love and rationalize separately, but the fact is, I didn't. Coming from forgiving her and myself for the situation to taking the blame was easy. It became natural for me to say, "It's my fault for not reacting better to the situation I'm in."

Can you blame yourself?

This is a commonly overthought question with a simple answer: "Yes." Why can't you? If it means that you will become a better person and be at peace with yourself, why won't you? People will say, "Why do you have to take the blame for something you didn't do?" They are right, you shouldn't. Nevertheless, how did you react to that situation that you didn't instigate? How were your emotions, and how well were your thoughts in sync with your logic when everything was said and done? Could you have prevented your anger? Could you have prevented the way you spat out hurtful words? Could you have placed yourself in a better position and learned from your lesson once all of this was over? Yes, yes, you can blame yourself.

Again, I'm not here giving you the necessities of life, rather I am giving you my life experiences and allowing you to view things from my perspective in hopes that you can relate and find peace within your life.

Who are you to not take blame for your life?

In the darkest of times, I sat back and pointed fingers as to why things weren't working out. I called out people on my mistakes and let them know it was their fault. I couldn't sit there and blame myself; there was no way. I created a bubble of hate in my life and knew that I was losing people around me. I knew I was broken, my relationships deteriorated, my mentality disintegrated, my money spent, my stamina low, and my lifestyle not where I wanted it to be.

I looked at the man in the mirror and realized the faults that were to blame had been right in front of me the whole time. I was staring at the only human in the way of me being great, the person who I needed to blame for all this, which I call a mess, was me.

But calling yourself a mess is only part of it. True story: not everyone who looks in the mirror is a mess or needs fixing. Chances are if you are content and happy with where you are now, the man in the mirror is the man you want to have reflected. Nothing can change where you want to be or who you are other than yourself and the blame you take for your own reflection.

When was the last time you looked at your reflection?

Skipping the routine that you are engulfed in is important to the journey where you can become successful, as this takes you out of your comfort zone. This comes with a lot of criticism, so be prepared for it. The friends or circle of individuals that surrounded you will be the first to criticize; however, every herd of animals needs a leader to create change.

I went into a very harsh spiral of the same routine in 2018. I was in a repetitive state of mind, and I found myself exactly where I was the year before with no advancement, no motives, no ambition and more importantly no purpose. When I looked in the mirror, I saw a man who had no idea what he was supposed to do on this earth. I slowly started to change my routine and allowed myself to fall back into my initial place of being. Regardless of whether or not this was accepted by others, it was a risk I had to take. I took blame for a lot of the things I had not wanted to and started to look at life in a different way. A very good friend of mine once told me that, "You have to get in the level of acceptance," and that was such an eye opener. It gave me the ability to accept the fact that the man in the mirror wasn't who I was or wanted to be, and I **accepted that.** The person I was looking at, the reflection staring back at me wasn't the man I had once known. My friend is a huge inspiration, and through his actions, allowed me to see acceptance in a very different way. The past is the past, and I couldn't do much about it other than to accept it and move on for the better.

We are taught to look at the past and see how far we have come, which as a concept, is fully flawed. We cannot look at the cup as half empty, and by looking at our past in comparison, we are doing exactly that. It is best that we look at where we want to be in the future and accept the fact that we are where we are today, with the potential for going where we want to go. Always look at where you want to be in the future and compare it to where you are today. The process of looking ahead rather than looking back at your past not only gives you immediate satisfaction, but subconsciously develops a thought process of independent positivity. I'm not saying it isn't healthy to remember where you came, from but rather than using that as fuel, think about what you can be and how much further you can develop.

What are you going to do today that will benefit your future reflection?

Will the man/woman in the mirror today be a different person in the future? Will you allow yourself the love and happiness that you require to be in full peace? When I say full peace, I mean knowing yourself. That comes at a price that you must be willing to pay, because believe it or not, every other person looking at their reflection is no different than you. The millionaires, the billionaires, the top 1% all bleed the same blood you do. So, what are you willing to sacrifice to become great and leave a mark on the human race?

There will be times when you will not be happy with where you are, and that is a good thing. The ups and downs of an emotional person are actually beneficial as they prove that the reflection is beyond a creature living on this earth. It proves that you are a human being, and that you feel. The knowledge that you need to change some of your bad habits is always a blessing.

Be careful of a dirty mirror.

Sometimes looking into a mirror and seeing your pure reflection can be convoluted, which means that your intentions and who you are can be masked by the poisonous surroundings. This does not make you evil or an unfulfilled human, rather it makes you shine through the issues of the society you live in. **Remember:** the beautiful lotus flower is found in murky waters. Sometimes in order to make a change you need to wipe the mirror clean of all its dirt, and that only happens with the small change or ripple of deeds that you are willing to produce.

The fact of the matter is, not all of us grow up looking at clean and clear reflections. Sometimes our reflections are complex, and within them we see the negatives imposed on us by society. Other times we see inspiration and what we are truly meant to be.

When Simba looked into the water and saw the reflection of his father, he realized that he needed to become the great integrity that filled Mufasa. Through trials and tribulations, he experienced a lot growing up; however, through the help of those who cared for him and who had the right intentions, his reflections began to showcase his own face. We all experience the trials of life, and they make us who we are, part of a story in this life that is temporary as we live to return the vessels (our bodies) back to earth. The story of the *Lion King* is such a lesson for us all at any age.

You can wipe the dirt off the mirror.

You don't have to worry about your past, where you were and came from. You may have made mistakes, and you may see that within your reflection, but are you going to allow your past self to determine who you are going to become in the future? Even if it is within you, your past life cannot tell the story of your future. It may depict your present, but it has no impact on the future YOU! Remember that it is okay to understand that where you come from shaped you into who you are today, but it is not an allowance of your energy to keep you where you were. It is fine to have pride in your past, pride in where you have come from and your journey until this day; however, looking at specific incidents that took so much negativity out of you will only have you in a state of regression.

I can look back at what happened, and I constantly do; it's only human that we are emotional. We, as humans, tend to always look for something wrong so we can fix it; meanwhile 50% of the time we are fine. I look back at my biggest loss in life, at my brother. That situation has had a toll on me until this very day. It has affected me in my daily activities along with my method of life. My reflections in the mirror are so pure with the positivity or negativity that follow me on a daily basis from that situation. But can I allow my past reflections to represent my future in a negative way? Sure, *if I allow them to*!

You must always see the cup half full.

My brother will forever be in my life, he will forever be in my heart, and there is nothing I can do to change the past. Therefore, my time cannot be spent contemplating what could have been. Rather, I take in my previous pain, reflection, and hurt, and I have decided to maximize my time here on this earth so that my future reflection has nothing but positive images from the past. Can you allow your reflection of yourself to be one that is to remain happy? Or do you constantly want to be in a state of soulful negativity?

Help is also there for you to ensure a more tasteful reflection. If you must stare at the person in the mirror, then by all means do so, but remember that your thoughts and ideologies are going to be seen by yourself.

At one point, I had to take care and control of who I was at that present moment, and it was only then that I noticed the man in the mirror was a different human being. My self-confidence was at an all-time low, and although people would think I was a very confident human being, deep down I was scared and couldn't think for myself to save my life. I started to realize that if I didn't become transparent toward the man in the mirror, I wasn't ever going to match my inner being with my outer image. I was real with myself; I began admitting my mistakes and shelling out anything that I did not want in my life. The biggest aspect that helped me change and become a better human being was the ability to be selfish with the man looking back at me. It wasn't that my love was not given to anyone, but rather I gave it to myself first. Beginning to fall in love with myself allowed me to wake up and look at myself in the mirror and to only realize that, hey, I am not my past, I am not even this moment. Rather I am who I want to be in the near future. Believe me when I tell you, you can wipe that dirty mirror and start over if you ever so choose. Your future depends on what you want to do today.

Be(come) the driver in your life.

When you envision yourself walking down the street, what is that you see? Do you see the faults and the imperfections that give you the absolute essence of life? Do you see how people see you? Or do you see a version of you that existed just for that split second? The truth is, you see what you feel, and you can sometimes control that, but what if your thoughts don't coincide with what your gut is telling you?

Towards the end of the court cases and my previous relationship I knew my gut was telling me one thing, but my reflection was telling me another. I lost control in what was an absolute necessary way in order to continue on. How could I have gained it back? What can I do to get back to the old me? (I speak about this in "Positive Vibes," where I indicate that my positive go-to is my motorcycle, and here we are again talking about it.) In order for my gut and my reflection be in tandem, I needed to clear my mind and get back to controlling my thoughts, my emotions, and my heart. The only way I know how to do that is to ride my motorcycle, and I mean ride for hours and hours on end with no real destination. I did just that. I remember when I first started to ride my bike, realizing that I had no control over where I wanted to go or what I wanted to do, but I knew one thing: I can control this bike.

At times I hated who I was becoming during the years leading up to 2020. When my brother passed away, I was forced out of the country for security reasons. I had to pack up and leave within 14 days of his passing, and I hated that I was not myself then. I remember waking up one of the days to shower and wash up before heading out to accept guests who paid their respects. I looked in the mirror and realized the life had been sucked out of me. My eyes were dry, there were bags under my eyes, my skin was pale, my hair was falling out, and my hands were so inflamed with eczema it was disgusting. I couldn't figure out who I had become and why I became this way. I kept talking to myself in the mirror as if I was talking to my brother, hoping that, at one point, I would be daydreaming, and all of this would end. I didn't know what to do or think, and I placed most of the blame on myself. I was hurting in ways that I didn't think I was able to, or that any human was capable of doing.

Once the burial occurred, we ended up going through a few days where we kept checking our phones to see if he had called. I didn't know what to do at times, and I remember hiding from everyone in the hallway outside and calling his number only to get a voicemail that wasn't set up. It was then that I really began to develop walls and the cold personality that I created from that moment. I remember there were a lot of people, faces I may have recognized, but what I was doing at the time was looking at each person to see if it was my brother. I grew angrier by the minute and was developing a mind that was suffocating itself in distrust. I couldn't trust a single soul but at the same time was searching for somebody I could confide in. What I didn't realize at the time was that this was my biggest lesson of life and one that was going to mold me into the man I am today.

As the days went by, I started to blame myself for all the misfortunes we went through. I would search for clues as to why it was my fault and what situations I could have changed to blame myself for them. I couldn't fathom the amount of pain my brother went through leading up to his passing, and that alone drove a pain of new color in me. Hung up on that night and the different things I could have done to save my brother, I held that for a long, long time. Was I a product of my surroundings? Yes, temporarily.

It's not that you shouldn't be in tune with your surroundings. You should. However, you must come to terms with how you are handling it. Going through the emotions of what is happening in your life at a set time is also beneficial for your mental health. Have you been able to accept what it is you are feeling at this exact moment? Do you accept that this situation you are dealing with is just temporary? The pain may last a lifetime, but you'll learn to live with it.

These were all questions I had to ask myself prior to engaging anyone else. See you really aren't your surroundings; you are who you surround yourself with. That is on both the mental and physical aspect of your life regardless of where you are. Whether it is the crowd you are hanging with that has a mentality of stagnancy or the area that you grew up in that does not have the standards you wish for, to achieve any type of growth, you must learn to cope with change. This change isn't one that is asked of you, and neither is it one that is found lying there for you to grab and embrace. Change occurs when you decide that you have outgrown the situation causing you a setback. Do you have a current situation holding you back? (Seriously, ask yourself and write it down). Now that you have thought about it, what about this situation is holding you back? Is it yourself, the person in the mirror? Your physical surroundings or your mental surroundings?

I knew at times that I was the one who needed to grab this change and entertain it for a while to see what type of results I encountered. It really wasn't easy at times, and it presented so many threats or obstacles. What was I supposed to do? Allow both my physical and mental surroundings to entertain my slow death? That is how I felt at times, as if I was living a slow death. See there wasn't anyone that I thought understood my pain or anyone who actually cared to help. At the time everyone was snooping to know what happened, and as vulnerable as I was at 21, I was still cautious. I remember walking home in Lebanon, and before I got to the gated community, I looked up to the balcony where my mom and I were living. I saw my mother standing there looking down to the street, and as far away as we were, I could see the tears drop from her face as she reminisced. I thought to myself, this is truly all my fault, and I was thinking of ways that would allow me to see my brother again. But you see, my surroundings weren't helping me understand another concept of thinking, and they weren't helping me change the life I was living; everything was temporary. Was it all my fault that this happened to me and that I was feeling this way? No.

Was I to blame that I wasn't doing anything about it to change my situation? Yes.

Recreating the image that you see in the mirror is paramount to becoming the next level of human. This recreation can take form in many ways regardless of the pain that you experienced or are experiencing. Companies and corporations do it when they realize that their brand isn't working as expected. Once the delegators within an organization realize that the work structure isn't at 100% efficiency, they restructure. This could be laying off individuals, moving individuals from different departments, and adding new members to the team. This is exactly how I envisioned my life and my mentality. I had to restructure, regroup, and change some things before they took hold of me and killed me off for good. This started with acceptance that I could not change the past, regardless of how much I cried and screamed. Was I to blame for it? I could sit here and lie to you, saying yes, I am to blame for it, but we both know there wasn't anything I could do to change the events of that night. I had to accept the fact that I was to blame if I remained stagnant and didn't change anything in my life to become better.

It was my mother who was the catalyst for this change. We sat at the dinner table in Lebanon one night, ready to eat. As we started, I could see her trembling and starting to cry before I even ate anything. What I didn't realize was that we had placed 4 plates on the table to accommodate my brother and father. At this time, it was just my mother and I living together. I didn't pay attention to the fact that my plate was covered in tears. I was crying without even realizing it. We got so frustrated with each other that we stopped eating and went out for fresh air. It was then that I realized I really needed to get stronger and change for her. I couldn't allow life to take its toll on my mom more than it already had. I was slowly becoming the driver in my life and taking a different road to success.

Sometimes you have to find the catalyst that will allow this change for your road to recovery. I had to begin to embody a change and realize that if I didn't change then I could actually blame myself for not doing anything about my problem. (A problem is only a problem if there is no solution for it, and almost 99% of the time, there is. So, don't lie to yourself about there not being a solution, because there is.) With this new change I needed to make, I realized that now was the time to blame myself. I needed to blame myself in a few ways that would catapult my new image into success. I needed to admit to myself that if I did nothing about how I thought or what was around me, I would not succeed. I began to admit to myself that I was wrong about my thoughts, wrong about the situation and how I went about it.

You see, most of the time, we are trapped in our ways, and we really get thrown into tunnel vision with the wrong ideologies. What we have thought to be right the whole time, most of the time just isn't. We won't ever know the difference unless we really step out of our comfort zone.

Embody the change you want now.

Currently, we are faced with so many questions about the future. You are faced with so many questions about the future that won't allow you to proceed. There are words, situations, instances, and social media posts that really do instill fear in us to stop us from accepting and adapting to change. Hey, if you're okay where you are and are not scared of staying in the same position all your life, kudos! But for those who want to truly make a change, the time for you to do it is always **NOW**.

Earlier I wrote about taking blame for your situations by yourself so that you can learn to forgive and forget. What I mean by forget is to really put forgiveness to the side once given. My situation with my brother's passing wasn't one I could blame myself for, but there are situations with people till this day in which I honestly can say that the blame is on me. We only get reactions from actions, and how people react is solely based on how we act towards them. (This is flawed if you have that one instance that is so out of line that you yourself are asking "What on earth is going on!?!")

How do I embody the change I want now? How can I become today what I envision for myself in the future? What is it I need to do to become great? Well, don't feel left out. We're all asking ourselves these questions. You have to find it in yourself first, the reason for change. Why is it that you want to change into something better? What's your motivation?

You really have to begin to define the reason for change. Understand that it will take a while, and through this time you will face your hardships. Friendships will be lost, relationships possibly ruined, and your old self will be tainted but all for the better. The decisions you make will affect your future; however, as I mentioned earlier, take the decision, and if it's wrong, take the blame and adjust to carry on. Stay woke to your surroundings and to the man in the mirror. Your reflection from where you are to where you will go is a true testament of acceptance of your past.

Become your future now.

Believe it or not, we all deal with the same issues whether we realize it or not. You may not think anyone understands what you are dealing with, but there are so many people just like you, who dress like you and who stress like you. Let's face it, most of the people living in North America today were probably brought here by immigrant parents who wanted a better future and hustled their way into the ranks of success. You think they were stuck in the past? Absolutely not. It probably fueled them to do better for their family. I doubt that any immigrant father blamed anyone other than himself for their problems or that he used that fire to create solutions for the family. They wanted to become their future now, regardless of the times.

I remember growing up, my father would always remind us to take responsibility for our actions, and to 'man up 'regarding whatever was happening. Nowadays this is labeled as verbal abuse by some household cultures; people are too soft. The generations where our parents placed us in check because they saw we were making mistakes at an early stage made us who we are now: grown, respectable, and honorable people.

Since you may have started thinking about the sacrifices your parents made for a better future for you, what sacrifices are you making? Are you still being weak by blaming others for your insubordination? Are you not acting on the things that have gone wrong in your life? You realize the bad relationships don't come from just you; they stem from others as well. But change starts with you. If we want to change the world, it starts with ourselves.

The man in the mirror is you; do you accept what you see?

Dirty reflections, clean images, actions that simulate thoughts … do you accept what you see? Nothing will improve without work. Nothing will change or become better without putting in effort. As you are, you are beautiful, and that beauty is defined as you see fit. Do not view yourself as someone who needs to change to commit to societal beliefs and values. The strongest and most admirable people are those who stick to their gut beliefs, the solid men and women of our times. It is important that we not get bullied into becoming a clone of what is around us.

So many of us have had amazing upbringings in which we were taught morals, respect, and honor by the generation that suffered to bring these guidelines to life. It's time that you look in the mirror and truly look deep into the reflection staring back at you. Look at what means the most to you, what standards are important to you, what you stand for and what you want to be remembered by. Do not for a second give that reflection the ability to play your past against you. You must understand, in order to move forward; you must accept responsibility for your actions and most importantly for *your life*. If the person in the mirror is who you want to see, then move on and become great. If the reflection isn't, and you want change, then wipe that mirror and start fresh.

Today is the day you become you again.

Exit Thoughts

I've really gone off the rails here. I started this chapter in 2017, I believe, and it took me around 3 years to finish it. You may think there isn't enough content, but when you really don't have inspiration to write or are going through things, it's tough. Dealing with the issues at hand that were developed over the years, I have always struggled with reflection. I tend to find the cringiest moments and replay them in my head, and it sucks. It sometimes also happens that I finish a conversation with someone and immediately regret how much I opened up to them. Someone told me it happens to them, too, so I guess I am not alone.

Through the years, I found that my reflection varied. It was always different at different stages of my life, and that was always confusing. It wasn't until this year, in 2021, that I realized that it was my stages of development. I had always found something wrong with the way I acted, moved, spoke, and held myself in situations. Then I began to realize a few things. For example, the outcome of almost every situation could have been different had I approached it in another manner. The ability to carry healthier relationships started with a healthier me, and the process of change in others began with the daily routines that I placed within myself. I guess we all would love healthier relationships with others, as loneliness kills, but sometimes, we forget about the healthier us. It's important that you wipe off the images of your past and create new reflections of your future. We tend to focus on the negatives instead of creating colorful pictures.

It was a rough time for me in the last couple of years, and I continuously used this method and adapt it to my daily life. I don't think I'll stop learning, and even in my thirties, I'm still reflecting on my daily actions with people. I am not looking at my past as motivation or inspiration, but rather looking towards the future at the improved me. Looking at the cup as half empty does nothing. But looking at it as a cup that is half full and knowing you can fill the rest and make it overflow is the key to creating a better and stronger you.

CHAPTER 6

Control

L ose control, gain control, and lose it again. A never-ending cycle, which is the root cause of our psychological problems, will continue as long as we embrace it. With social media coming to a peak, our minds are embedded with "Do better" and "You can be better" memes and tags. This isn't giving us motivation but rather allowing us to lose control over our lives, as we strive to fill the void created by subliminal mishaps to gain notoriety.

Losing control, not being sure of what your thoughts are ... no thanks. I for one want to be the captain of my own ship. This is not to be misconstrued with simple tasks, such as being the passenger in a vehicle or choosing what to eat, but rather

94

the bigger issues in life. You may conform and compromise to others' standards, but this can only happen if you are truly in control of your life in all other aspects.

I often ask myself, is *insecurity a futile imitation of our confidence in shadow form?* What we don't portray to the public is that we often hide in the darkness of our own realm. What defines our reality are thoughts that we keep to ourselves, and that we do not bring into existence. This is in **your control**. Whether you decide to allow that control to become negative or to remain positive is entirely up to your choice. What your mind speaks is separate from the world, which will allow you to fix onto the dream of reality, meaning that what you allow yourself to think will essentially become your physical surroundings. The word "manifestation" is strong, yet it can only be as strong as the light in your darkness that follows your every step. Where are you walking in your mind and soul?

Let's look at your personal life in 5 different ways, the same ways I look at my life and that helped me get through it all.

Call it the 5 fingers of control.

The Thumb

Let's face it: what on earth do you use your thumb for the most? Giving people a reaction of either thumbs up or down, right? How often do you give yourself that thumb up or down? Being in control of your mind set and your energetic vibe is so important, it's ridiculous. People don't see it and tend to forget about this pillar that holds all the other 5 fingers together. Without the thumb, the hand will have a hard time holding and keeping a grip of things.

The things that your hands embrace are the essentials of your life, and you will at times not even notice them. People will always have a hand outstretch for help, and it is within your power to either embrace this energy or deny it. This simple rule ties in perfectly with every finger on the hand. Your reaction to this exact thing is crucial and will be determined by your thumb. The energy requested is reciprocated by the energy within you and given off by your thumb.

Try practicing the 'thumbs up' rule.

The rule states that on any occasion, when faced with adversity, always give yourself the thumbs up, whether mentally or physically. If you're at an impasse and are very indecisive, give yourself the thumbs up for feeling that exact way and continue on. If you have made a mistake, challenge your mind to give itself the thumbs up so that you may continue on with the lesson learnt rather than the mistake and its consequences. Your ability to train your mind to be disciplined in this manner can only be achieved by following the first couple of chapters in this book. You're going to realize that the thumbs up rule follows the "as you are, you are beautiful" ideology.

It's fine to mess up, and it's fine to be okay about it. It's fine to have flaws, and it's fine to be okay about it. Your recognition of the flawed and indefinite should be clear, and that will only be possible when your soul, mind, and physicality are aligned. People and their opinions are alike in that we've all got them. Now here's where the thumbs up rule comes in handy.

My mother taught us to not argue with an idiot.

At times it's better to agree than to argue; this couldn't be truer. Sometimes the opinion of the individual at the other end of the conversation can be so daft that you may feel like you have lost total control. Regain control of your feelings, emotions, mental thoughts, and physical ability by giving that human being a thumbs up. Gain control; don't lose it. If you do want to argue with an idiot, then you better come with the time to waste, the facts to prove them wrong, and most importantly your image, which you may or may not tarnish because of this fool's thoughts.

After the passing of my brother, we as a family encountered everything from rumors to lies to deception. We sat and listened, but because we knew the truth, it was easier to give the thumbs up, as we decided not to argue with idiots. At times we couldn't obey this rule because our emotions were in play, and it was hard to control them under these circumstances. This is where you will notice the middle finger coming in, a key piece of keeping your cool. Sometimes with the thumbs up you also have to raise your middle finger and not care what anyone says or thinks.

Getting or giving the thumbs up to situations can take you a lot of places but only the places you want to point to. Life is not what it was 15 years ago; I believe we can all agree on that. It has become dangerously exploitable, and we are the subjects of its exploitation. The norm of living in a positive environment is now motivation rather than second nature. Of course, we still have those individuals who are positive and whom we may see on a daily basis, but let's read the second page. Following what is required to be positive is the knowledge of the negativity around us that we have embodied at times. We resort to signs, pictures, images, and people, to manifestos that allow us to stimulate the enzymes within our souls to release positive thoughts into our minds. As a human race, we have allowed symbolism to rule the way we visualize these moods. When you think of positivity, what is it that you symbolize? The one symbol that gives it away is the thumb, aka a thumbs up.

Because we no longer live in an untroubled world, it is important that we try to maintain control of a positive mindset. We cannot control all that happens in our lives, but we do have control over what we think and how we bring it to life. The problem with this type of control nowadays is that there are too many distractions that alter the road our life takes. It isn't your fault or mine but rather time. With the advancements we have made as human beings, life is so much more accessible and easier that we do not know what to focus on anymore, and the simple thought of control has now diminished. We no longer have the ability to focus, and if we do it's for a very short period of time. Technology has created an over-socialization of information at our fingertips, and that has overloaded our mental capacity and caused a lack of focus and confusion. Can you focus on the ability to grow the strength of your mindset? What are you dedicating your thumbs up to? Why is it when someone gives you a thumbs up, you feel good? Do you feel as if you are in control of your emotions towards others when you give a thumbs up to someone? Is it possible that we can actually control the positive recurrence to our brains so that it becomes second nature?

My mindset has become faceted with different sabotaged topics created by the media and the distractions around me. I have gone from having a great day to becoming extremely anxious the next. I have found that my anxiety has developed in large clumps over the years to the point where I have developed an allergy to normalcy.

Prior to 2011, I never really had anxiety, never really developed a definition of what anxiety meant. Neither had I known what panic attacks were, nor had I ever had one. The developments of my depression, anxiety, and panic attacks started developing the day of January 24, 2011. I started thinking negatively, which created a bubble of distrust in society and began my life as a singular entity. My thumbs up mentality became a thumbs down, and it really did change my mindset.

I was always the individual who was positive and hustled my way into whatever it was that I wanted. I imagined the future of the economy, I imagined myself as a 5-year success and had no false sense of security. When 10:30 p.m. hit on January 24, 2011, I began losing control of trust in society, and my mind became uncontrollably confused. You must understand, I saw no positivity in having my brother pass away in my arms or hearing my parents crying.

Any time I was able to have the thumbs up mentality, we would end up back in court, and I would listen to my 911 call that would send me back into such a distilled cup of heartache. Somehow, I found my mind getting stronger during the case, and the ability to forfeit these thoughts were then developed through the images of my mother and father. As I was a witness, I had to give my testimony of that night. I remember before providing my testimony I would look over to my mom, and she would give me the thumbs up as a sign to stay strong. I would look back and realize that both my parents were so broken with rage and sadness that they forced themselves to stay strong for me and Shadi.

Regulating your mind to stay in the thumbs up mentality is not an easy task. This requires your ability to push through your puzzled thoughts to find the ones that allow you to think positive and to gain control of your mind once again. Giving yourself the thumbs up on a regular basis will allow you to not only feel accomplished but to gain the trust of your confidence once again. This finger of control is the first step in regaining the trust your energy needs.

Gain your confidence at any cost.

The term "fake it till you make it" may play a part in your life, but it shouldn't here. It is difficult to understand negativity if we do not live through it to appreciate its counterpart. If you start with yourself, by gaining the momentum to change the thumbs down to a thumbs up in your life, I promise you, you will slowly regain the first step toward having control of your life. Find a reason behind your thumbs up, a reason to gain the trust of your peers, and the capability to channel your truest self. If you must practice in the mirror, do it. Your reflection will be the kindest and most sincere while the world waits for the privilege of *your experience*.

The Index

The finger that dictates where you want to go based on your decisions and consequences will forever be your index finger. "Point at the suspect," or "What would you like from the menu?" or "Which of these do you want? Please point."

The fact is that we use our index finger for a lot in our life, and we take it for granted all the time. What happens after we point impacts us in ways that we would never think possible. Think about this the next time you point at something and how the aftereffect of pointing changes your life.

This plays two parts: where you want to go and the blame game. Is it possible that both are able to coexist within the same sentence when applying it to our lives? Yes. Think about it: if you can index the reason to blame and how you want to achieve the ability to fix the future, wouldn't that be having them both in the same sentence? Taking the blame for the actions of others is not what I am saying but rather achieving the self-realization that you are to blame as well. Every action establishes a reaction of greater or equal force. Do you have the ability to blame once reacted to?

That's the power of the index finger that I want to write about. You have the power to point to the path you want to travel and to control what happens to you. If someone asks what it is that you want, you point at it. Remember this however: the instant you choose in that specific moment is your right decision. What happens next is the exact result of your decision during that time, and you must know that you cannot change or regret the choice you made. If you point at a big decision, make sure that when you do you take the choice you have pointed to, you choose it fiercely. Raise your head up, allow your thoughts to be simple, with no reasoning other than the decision you chose, and go ahead with it.

This second finger of control can be loosely used; however, be careful, as even that has consequences. When combined with the truth or a lie the index finger can manage to either create or destroy a life. You're no different from the other human being attempting to hustle into happiness or for happiness. Although I am my father's successor, I found myself giving my father advice at one point. We had a conversation, and he had indicated to me that maybe the decision he made in the past (coming to Canada) was not a good idea. In an attempt to reassure him, I found myself at the cusp of saying, "It's okay. It's a beautiful country. You made the right decision." However, I did not. Instead, I asked him, "At the time of your decision in the early 90s, when you decided to come here, was that the right decision?" With no hesitation he said, "Yes, but ..." His answer was a strong-willed "yes" was followed by a hesitation. This hesitation was what life played itself out to be and what this country made it for him. We cannot as human beings be mad at the fact that life played itself out to be what it is unless we had a hand in it.

A pointed choice today has a ripple effect for our future, forever.

Battling the ups and downs of life that come when we point toward decisions, we make is only half the battle. The decisions made today also have a huge impact on how things pan out for you, and you may have already known this, but it's good to hear it once more. You may think that the decision you make isn't as important, or you may downplay it, but you're hurting yourself more than anything. I have downplayed decisions thinking they won't be that big of a problem, and a year down the road, I am suffering from the consequences of my choices.

It's fine, though; know that if you lose the control that you once had, you can gain it back. Get back to what made you who you are. We all have it in us to make something major happen, and we usually steer off that path with comfort. Don't let that get the best of you.

I've done it to myself, because I allowed myself to work on other goals rather than focus on finishing mine. This has not only led me to falling into depression but also delayed the process of my goals materializing. This could be in the form of a relationship or everyday issues that you may deal with, but the truth of the matter is only you can control your situation.

I used to have the victim mentality and in a lot of instances I still do. I am attempting to run away from that mentality because it isn't right. Taking control isn't being in control all the time; that's unhealthy. Rather, it's the decisions you make for yourself without outside influence. Rid yourself of social media, outside opinions and social media advertisements, and focus on what's needed to gain back that positivity of control.

A good leader is always in control but the team they lead does not feel controlled. If a boss controls and the team feels as if it's being micromanaged, it leads to a negative or disruptive feeling. Now the team doesn't have to be a team you are leading, but rather those around you that you take care of or are a part of.

Control, however, is so much further than your ego or pride may assume. It is the concept of truly having the discipline to **resist temptation**, whatever that may be. My control was so far gone that I lost the mere existence of discipline, and I allowed outside influences to filter their way into my life. Now should I have allowed that? Absolutely not, but as humans we have our moments of weakness, and when we do, we allow these influences to walk into our lives and, at times, all over us. On any normal, confident, clear sky day we would not allow this foolishness to happen, but it is only when we are most vulnerable or feel as if we are about to lose something so valuable that we become weak. The joke is on us though; if we're meant to lose it or if it loses interest, it will leave. This only leaves us in a state of insecurity and diminished self-confidence that won't allow us to grow.

I write to you from experience. I promise I am not hypothetically preaching ideas about what I think people go through. My recent breakup is a prime example of exactly what I am speaking about. During one point in the relationship, I came to the realization that it might have been all that I had ever been praying for, and that it was too good to be true. Now at first, I didn't think much of how it would make me feel, but once I realized that it was this amazing love, I started to lose control of my consciousness and the ability to control my thoughts. I was no longer disciplined, rather I was a victim of this love and a slave to my insecurity. That is a trait and flaw of mine that I have realized needs work.

I have come to the terms that the discipline needed wasn't the restraint given at the time. My insecurity played a huge role with the problems faced as a couple, and this wasn't due to the lack of control only but to the lack of thought control. I wasn't pointing the finger at myself anymore; in fact, I wasn't even pointing any fingers at anything. I was too focused on the fact that it may be too good to be true to the point it became just that.

A piece of advice I want to give you as the reader: do not be consumed by love if the outcome is insecurity. Allow yourself to feel the love for yourself and the love for your partner. Indicate where the boundaries are that you can share and allow it to prosper on its own. If you are to control anything in love, control your actions towards your partner but not the love itself. You mustn't cage a bird, and never pick a daisy out of a flower bed. You must allow both to fly and flourish within their respective fields, so that you can enjoy the beauty that life brings.

I knew I needed work, and it's in the power of the index. Have you been able to point at something in your life that needs work? I created the 5 fingers of control concept to help remind me of what I am able to do, think, act, and see as a human being. I knew that there were categories of my mental control that can be found within the palm of my hand. Each finger represents a different subject and topic of control that affect us on a daily basis. Realizing that the index was my second step to truly mastering the world in the palm of my hand, I was able to point out the areas that needed work, to the blame I take on myself for situations I could have acted on better, the future goals I needed to work on, and most importantly back at my old self, to where I was and where I never wanted to return.

The Bird

Have you ever flipped anyone off? Sometimes it gives you pure satisfaction, doesn't it? Sometimes it calms anger and other times it's pure comedy. Nonetheless the 'middle finger' is one of the most important gestures out there in today's world. Figuratively speaking, this finger allows you to go through your life with a fine-tooth comb and with the raise of one finger, change it for better or worse.

Most of us are living with this self-conscious feeling of judgement that hangs above us. When you raise your middle finger in confidence you realize one of two things: either you know you're in trouble, or the new you that you've discovered is trouble—good trouble.

We seek the ability to know ourselves and in the process of knowing ourselves we sometimes lose those around us. The ability to just be ourselves, from the day we are born to the day we die is a complex action. We are loosely judged by our actions and sometimes by our past but never by the ability that we hold, which is that we can change our future.

It's also important to recognize that one should consider the road that can be travelled rather than the road that is traveled. The ability to raise your middle finger, yet still care about those around you, is a concept that is so hard to grasp sometimes, yet it is so simple. If you are no longer living for others but rather living for yourself, those around you start realizing the care that you may be able to give them. I'm not saying be a total jerk, but I am saying be a little selfish with your time, because no one is going to really do that for you. *Do not raise your middle finger in a state of aggression but rather in a state of total calm*. You need to be really level-headed when you realize that the life that you currently have will only be affected by the mentality that you will develop.

Over the years I've been in situations where it was very hard for me to grasp the concept of being selfish. Being selfless is always a great thing, but later down the road you start realizing that you lose yourself before you lose anybody else. It is also important to reflect on the situations that require you to not care, because those situations are impactful to your life.

When my brother passed away, I moved into a transient form of life that gave me more of what I didn't want. I stopped talking, I stopped asking, I stopped responding to individuals, and most importantly I stopped caring about anything and everything that was around me. You have to understand the period of me losing my brother developed the trauma that I wouldn't deal with until later. When I grew up, and I got a little older and matured, I began to realize the negative impact of me raising my middle finger at that time. The trauma that you deal with sometimes will affect you today and can affect you tomorrow, but most important is to realize today that you're affected, so that your tomorrow is a healthy one.

Everything that surrounds us now, from technological advancements to social media and how the world works, plays a pivotal role in how we view ourselves and most importantly each other. Society will give you an image and opinion that may or may not coincide with your true values. At the time you may find yourself brushing these opinions away and making sure that they don't affect you. The truth is these social media sites and advancements are doing a little bit more than just showing us images, quotes, and ideas of how life is. Our subconscious is absorbing so much more information than we are on a daily basis, more than we even know. It really is a fight between our subconscious and our conscious.

Chances are if you come from a traumatic experience in your life, people are going to judge regardless of the position you are in. You really need to realize that the judgment comes from a place of misunderstood conclusions, a place of pure judgment, and most importantly a place from not living through the trauma that you have. After 2011, I began to realize that it was tough for me to open up to people only because I knew people could not understand my situation or what I was dealing with. Who was I going to open up to, who was I going to talk to, if all they knew was the outside story? I didn't believe anyone would actually view or understand my pain and the loss I had suffered.

As a family we went through a time where we saw judgment, and we began to fight this judgment on a daily basis as if fighting trolls on a post off the internet. We continuously fought our way through and replied to every individual comment that came at us about the situation. After a while it was clear as day that we needed to flip the bird to almost anyone and everything that didn't serve us in a healthy way.

Of course, flipping the bird in this context is a metaphor for not caring, and if you know the truth, the not caring part is easy. In none of these cases do I actually or have I actually flipped the bird to someone. For me, the middle finger is a metaphor to understanding myself and not caring what others may think is the truth.

Now you can only imagine the type of side effects that came with the way that we lost my brother and the way that the whole situation happened. Not only was I beginning to care about opinions in how society portrays me, but I began to distrust everything around me. From the simplest thing, like trusting that my mail would arrive on time, to not telling my secrets to anyone. It's crazy to say that after 10 years I am still sometimes facing the same issue, the issue of my distrust in society. If I was able to continuously flip the metaphorical bird, I'd do anything and everything around me in a self-confident way, and I think I would be more at peace than the chaos that currently runs through my heart and my mind. I'm not perfect; I still have my days where I hit a blocked wall and I fall back two steps behind the advancement that I made the day before. One thing that I have learned is that as long as the truth is known and you have it within you, your truth is your actual weapon, and no other opinion should really matter.

I think my anxiety at times is heightened because of public perception of myself and the public perception that is bestowed upon those around me. What is it that I can do to change that? Is it really in my control, or should I even remotely think about controlling the public perception of myself by fighting the truth that they know? This could be applied in many ways regardless of the situation, the relationships, whether business or personal, friendships or family relationships.

One thing that I have realized over the years is that sometimes it is better to keep your silence rather than deal with the fight that you must put up. Essentially you would be flipping the bird if you keep your silence, because you would not be fighting back a public perception of you that is flawed. Your resilience towards the truth that you know to be accurate will give you the confidence that you need in order to move on from the situation that you're dealing with.

I encountered this exact problem when I was going through my relationship breakup, my friendship losses, my business relationships, my work relationships, and most importantly the relationship I have with my parents. I'm not saying I don't care and live in a carefree world but rather have my care dedicated to those who matter. I have begun to realize that the energy that I put out is sometimes not the energy that I get back, and I have to be okay with that, because the confidence that I have in myself should suffice.

Imagine being accused of something that you did not do, something that places you in guilt's sway or rather ruins your reputation. Your first step would be defending and trying to fight for the truth. You actually wouldn't be fighting for the truth; you would be trying to fight to convince the individuals of the actual truth. Meanwhile the individuals that you're speaking to are in a different mindset. The energy that you will waste to continuously defend yourself by trying to convince someone of something (who either has already moved past it or does not have the empathy required to understand your situation) is pointless. Most of us are only fighting for a place in someone's life if we are truly breaking down.

I was accused of multiple things over the course of the last 10 years, regardless of what type of relationship I was in. Just recently I was accused of a situation that was part of a relationship that I recently got out of, and at that moment, it had played a role that angered my emotions. It truly did set me off balance. When the individual told me about what it was that they accused me of, I was furious. I know it to be—deep in my heart—that I was not the individual to do what they had said of me. But it soon came to light, and I had to understand that regardless of how many years of friendship or love someone may have with you, it's the lack of empathy that people have that destroys the ability to understand you.

As I'm writing this, I am thinking of that exact situation, and although my emotions fluctuate, I am placed in a whirlpool of feelings. I always resort back to the truth in my heart that I know to be obedient to the laws that I live by. I understand I am not perfect, and I am not an individual who is a complete human being, but I also understand that I need to fight to be alive. After I calmed down and understood the situation, I realized that the individual spoke to me out of frustration and anger. The other traits that this individual embodied while they were admitting how they felt about the relationship was the lack of communication that they have.

Understanding what was happening, I had to flip the situation, the bird. I was not flipping the bird to the individual, but rather to the actual situation that was causing me anxiety, from the moment we hung up the phone to the moment that I am writing this. I had to stop caring about what the topic was and how it hurt me, because deep down, I knew the truth. I knew what was happening.

Through the ability to not care about others' opinions comes the ability to forgive but not forget. Most of us forgive others in response to an apology for what wrong they have done us.

Can you forgive without an apology?

This is a form of control that you can create for yourself that will give you the ability to grow your confidence. As I mentioned, forgiveness usually comes in response to an apology or an admission of guilt. Yet rarely do we forgive ourselves. This type of forgiveness is one that is given to someone with no conversation, no apology, or no intent of apologizing.

Can you forgive someone that has done you wrong without them apologizing? This type of control is associated with the idea of flipping the bird and using your middle finger for your own protection. When you stop caring about the opinions of others and truly realize the confidence you have in yourself, forgiveness is easy. Not only will this allow you the confidence you need but also the closure to move on from the situation holding you back.

Most of us seek an apology for the way someone has treated us, so that we can attempt to move on and find new beginnings. This is not the case. Since my brother's passing, I heard a lot of rumors and anger from close family members and friends, including things that should have never been said as they would eventually hurt my family. Half the time I didn't have the energy to confront everyone, but I always had it in heart that I wanted to. I slowly began to realize that in order for me to move on and hold no hate in my heart, I needed to forgive. I slowly began to forgive people who hurt me without even speaking to them about the situation.

Even with my relationships, I used to look for closure to help me with moving on. I quickly learned that people have their own opinion regardless of how wrong they can be. Their own portrayal of the relationship can never change as long as they think they have done nothing wrong. I started forgiving with no conversation and realizing that the love I had for them shouldn't change. They may have done me wrong, but they didn't know any better at the time. People may not know how to love us, and we can't hold that against them. They may not have realized how to love themselves let alone how to allow the love to reach us.

This is the strength in the middle finger symbolism. It's the ability to hold confidence in the truth regardless of society's opinion. It's learning to care for those around you yet always pursue a life of your own choice. It's the ability to forgive without conversation in order for your own preservation.

The 'I Do"

Is there control in love? Should you control the relationship or allow it to flow? Do you think that if you let it flow naturally you would actually be under the control of love? Some may say it's redundant, but there is so much control in everything that embodies *love.*

From the moment we start falling in love to the day we stand across from our partner to say our vows, we allow ourselves to become vulnerable. Our vulnerability is what controls us, what allows us to become captives to this love. This doesn't necessarily need to be understood in a negative manner, as the idea of companionship is subjective. Those who have been happily in love will define it as the best type of captivity they have been in. That type of control is fully acceptable to them but may not be someone else's view. Some individuals may say marriage and love is similar to a prison, whilst others define it as the best-kept secret or the one thing that has been the missing piece in their life. This is the reason why I explained that the idea of love or love itself is individualistic.

We can either see it as being positive or negative but that transformation into love is dependent on events created. None of us really planned to fall in love or rather pick a human being and purposely fall in love with them. We don't wake up one morning and say I'm going to be falling in love with this person today, and I'm going to spend the rest of my life with them. What ends up happening is an understanding between souls, hearts, and minds over a period of time by two people. The interest leads to conversation, which leads to going out, which leads to intimacy, which leads to the knotting of hearts. Love doesn't have a timeline, and I personally do not believe that we should place a specific time for when we should fall in love.

That old school love still exists.

I genuinely believe in generational love. Love exists in different eras and also changes every couple of decades. And the love that our parents had during the Baby Boomer era or the 50s and 60s might no longer exist. It may exist, and it may be available to some individuals, but that is a rarity.

The access to the ideas of moving on or the ability to just fall in love with another individual is so easy nowadays that we truly do not have control over it. If one relationship doesn't work out, we'll move on to the next one; and if that one doesn't work out, there will be one after that. The options are numerous, hence the reason most couples don't fight to keep what they have regardless of the troubles they are facing.

There is no age limit that an individual has to have in mind when they want to settle down. The ideas of building a home and starting a life with someone can be defined in so many different ways. I myself have experienced this over the last 10 years in various forms. I have been in relationships that have had the mentality of settling down at that exact moment and some that didn't want to settle anytime soon. It could be that you have not yet found the one who is willing to take that extra step, but we'll never know until it happens.

Remember that you are not your old love.

Through the last decade I had been introduced to a few heart breaks, and I myself have broken a few hearts. I think it's only healthy that we look at ourselves in true, honest fashion. My most recent heartbreak is one that I thought to be "the one." I write about certain situations within the last decade that caused me to fall in love or rather to know when the falling was occurring.

I had spent almost 2 years with one individual, and I'd be lying to you if I said I wasn't head over heels for her. The type of love that made me think of doing everything with her and considered her emotions, amongst other things, before I considered my own. I risked it all—I mean all of it—when it came to her. I really wanted to control my past mistakes in this relationship. I did not want to commit the same mistakes with her, as she made me want to become a better man. As that man, I had experienced a lot before I met her or was even introduced to our love. The reason I was single was because of past relationships that didn't work, and from them I took valuable lessons. When we first started dating, I vowed not to act on the same mistakes.

My trust in society was at a pivotal point as well. I had been hurt multiple times over; therefore, this emotion did not come overnight but rather it took me some time to build trust with her. It was over the period of a few months that I had determined she wasn't another drifter in my life who would be here today and gone next Monday. I decided that with this girl, I would be my naked-soul self. I would open up about everything in my life, apologize first, give before I received, and value her friendship before anything else. I took this risk and I do not regret it for a moment, as it allowed me to learn that I can be myself regardless.

I knew I was in control the moment I was able to correct my present actions and no longer be the person that I was. It wasn't easy, and I would have an inner battle with myself all the time about what and how I wanted to be. My friends would tell me to be patient; however, I didn't want her realizing she was with someone who was not an open book with her. Even though the relationship did not work due to circumstances, I am perfectly fine with the way I had given her my whole self. The idea of building walls and not being 100% with a partner didn't make sense at that time, and it will never make sense to me.

Become an open book with your lover.

Getting over the love that you never wanted to let go of may be one of the hardest things to control. The subliminal 'I do' that we act on in a relationship goes a long way in the love category. Letting go of hurt love is not as hard as some may think, as the hurt eventually takes over the love that was once shared. When things are normal and the love is strong, letting go is such a difficult task. I have been a witness and a victim to both these break ups, one where problems caused a breakup and one where the circumstances caused the split.

When hurt takes over, the mentality during the initial stages of a breakup is pure pain. Images and caches of negative events may even pop into your mind and will cause you to want to distance yourself. This may be a form of control that you can place yourself in to help with the demise. If the breakup has occurred and the hurt is present, distance yourself. Believe me when I tell you, the distance will help more than it will do damage. If there are no hurtful circumstances that caused the breakup, but rather situational issues that have caused you to leave, that's where your own strength should be summoned. Letting go of the individual you love and the future you envisioned with them, for no reason other than outside circumstances, is a different type of hurt.

Have you been in a position where you can relate to what I am saying? It is not easy giving up your heart. Is it giving up, though? Maybe this love of yours that you're letting go of now isn't for you at this present moment but will be yours in the future. It could possibly be the right person but wrong timing.

Well, how do you control that type of "letting go?" It is totally up to you. What I did to get through my heartbreak was to let go and let God. This was by far my hardest break up, one that I least expected. As you read this, I am currently going through it. In a way I am bringing this to you, the reader, in a very raw fashion.

I have decided to let things flow naturally and not force anything into existence. Grasp the idea of controlling the 'I do' that you once gave to yourself to never humiliate, disrespect, or dishonor yourself. It is important you remember this; I am currently trying to exemplify this as well.

Even though I am aching to reach out to the individual I once was in a relationship with, I am forcing myself not to. You cannot be the one who continuously reaches out to them when the individual has asked for their space of healing. You must realize that, in reality, people are selfish with the way they do things. It is important that you control this part of your life. Becoming selfish with your time and how you get over things is a proud moment that should be embraced on all fronts. Do not take away from the love you once had, and make sure you grow an appreciation for the time spent together. Control your hate, even deplete it if you have to.

When controlling your breakup is dependent on the other individual's actions, you are not in control. The 'I do' that you once gave to yourself to always love yourself is slowly diminishing. You are placing your emotional future in another human's hands, and that gives them the control that you ache for. You're not alone, because this feeling of neglectful love is experienced by so many people in this world. Unrequited love is by far the hardest. At times we give others love that is meant for us, love that we create for ourselves.

The thinking that we are undeserving of love because we haven't found the right one yet is unhealthy. Turning sorrow into thoughts of happiness isn't easy, however, it is achievable. When we are single, we are taught to love ourselves and learn who we are so that when it's time, we find those who are also on the same wavelength. *Give yourself a vow*, a set of vows, if you want, *to always love yourself to the furthest extent possible, and when it's time to love someone else, that you give that person all the love you are capable of giving*. Your 'I do' to yourself is as important as air is to your lungs. Control your inner love and control your thoughts towards yourself so that you can love others effortlessly.

Memories are made through growing love.

Growing older, I realized that love is ever-changing. It can grow old with you or against you, but that is up to your destiny (if you believe in destiny). Part of controlling love is allowing love to flow naturally.

I remember a time when I wanted to control every little aspect, forgetting that I really should only focus on the important elements. I think over-controlling things in a relationship, to the point where you are focused on making things work, works against you. You can't be attached to the point that you have a fear of loss. You must learn to have confidence that what is meant for you will be yours.

This ability to let go and allow the future to play out is paramount. Not only will this allow for the safe arrival of what's meant to be in your life, but it will also allow for what's not meant to stay, to leave you alone. Maybe allowing your love to grow itself is the control you require.

The Pinky

Probably the most important finger and yet the smallest finger of them all is the pinky. Representing respect, loyalty, and honor, it holds the most weight in life. Respect is defined in every aspect of our life, but every situation requires a different type of respect. This is probably the easiest to control yet the most complicated of the 5 fingers. Raising the level of respect and honor that you may have for people starts with yourself. Usually taught through generations, these three have existed and will continue to be passed on.

We've seen these three items in movies through the years. They have taught us different lessons, yet they all refer to controlling your inner self. Because we wouldn't know respect if we weren't cognizant of our own actions. We wouldn't know honor if we didn't respect our words. We wouldn't know loyalty if we didn't combine the two and stay true to ourselves. Think about it: you constantly give your word to people, regardless of the subject. Through promises and other methods of reassurance, you begin the process of attaching respect, honor, and loyalty to your name. Think about your day-to-day actions and responsibilities; how many times are you actually defining how people respect you and how honorable your word is?

I have spoken about the first 4 fingers of control, but they are truly dependent on the responsibility the last one holds.

Since we are only here for a short time, it is important that we hold our legacy close to us. For when we leave this earth, we leave behind only our reputation and legacy that we built. I will speak on the different types of respect you can either give or receive and how it is implemented through the different fingers before I start relating it to my personal situations.

You, the reader, are capable of being the greatest version of yourself. Do not for a second think that you can't achieve any of these rules or believe that you cannot become one of the greatest. It is all possible; however, it starts with your mentality and respecting your mind. How people perceive you is directly related to how you perceive yourself. The moment you walk into a room, your impression is felt and that can go a long way. That is why the pinky is the most important of them all.

Controlling your personal respect can be applied against different areas of your life. The words spoken about yourself will allow your subconscious to build the self-confidence you need. People will see this respect without you realizing it. Do not overdo it though; respect yourself without the ego.

What you do in private will dictate how you hold yourself in public. If you respect yourself enough to take care of your personal hygiene in private, you will be noticed in public outings as a person of clean etiquette. The way you speak of your persona will direct how people see you and treat you. If you ever begin to lack self-confidence, look back at the 5 fingers of control and start regaining your life. We are surrounded by negativity and situations that alter our thoughts. As much as we stray away from our uniqueness, we will always resort back to ourselves. No one really understands you like you do. So why disrespect yourself if you know it's only you in the end?

Controlling respect in relationships—now that's where it is most important. Do not ever burn a bridge regardless of how bad it needs burning. You may encounter relationships that require you to walk away from them, but whatever you do, ***always leave with respect***.

What people can't take away from you is a good deed. I have always been asked why I am the way I am with people regardless of how well or poorly they treat me. It's a very easy and simple formula that I follow: do unto others as you want yourself to do to you. This again, as repetitive as it may be, goes back to treating yourself with respect first. If you can hold your head high, knowing that your actions have expressed the respect you wanted, you should be happy that your reputation is building itself.

Can I force love?

You can try to control it, but good luck if you want it to last! You can't control something that comes naturally and creates a bond between two people. Either it builds itself and flows naturally, or you attempt to control the build and watch it crumble miserably.

You see, I have been in relationships in the past where I knew I had to control it and have things my way. This was a very poor way of thinking as the relationships became very toxic due to my ego and pride. I thought that as a man I needed to control my emotions and the situations I am in. When I say control, I mean not letting anyone in and building that wall. I did so many times over and found myself achieving the same results. I had lost my brother, left countries, been talked poorly about, betrayed, and forcefully shamed with how I lived my life. So, blame me if you must, but I couldn't trust anyone.

When I started building these walls, I noticed I was hiding behind the true emotion that I was so eager to let out. Sometimes this played out in my favor, as the women I dated would not stick around for long due to incompatibility. I knew I couldn't control someone walking away or whether or not we were compatible for each other. What I could control is the ability to knock down my walls and let someone in. This was my form of respect towards the relationship.

Prior to 2011, it was easy for me to let people in; however, I started building walls the moment I discovered the betrayal my brother faced. I guess it really hurt me and that I took that hurt with me everywhere that I went. There were times when I couldn't control the wall-building, and I hurt people who that didn't deserve it. I realize I am human, and I make mistakes; however, through my life, I have concluded that in order to be defined as human, I need to be openly vulnerable. I can control that.

Growing up I was exposed to both the corporate and the street hustle. I was able to see the type of respect given in professional deals and everyday trades. I began to realize that it really is the human that places this precedence of honor rather than the deal at hand. When one of us gave our word during a street deal, we knew that we had to honor it regardless of what we were dealing with on a personal level. It was a simple handshake that we gave that sealed any deal during my time.

Now, if you didn't honor your word, your street cred was tarnished. The more you dishonored your word on the street, the less business you had or were able to drum up. The word on the street held so much more power than the truth, as the masses believed the majority rather than the truthful minority. We were able to grow up and realize the meaning of loyalty. The evidence is that the relationships we had built in the 90s still exist to this day.

The corporate world is a little different in all 3 aspects. Once you enter the field you will realize that your respect is honored when you deliver the word you gave management or your team. Your resume really does become, "What have you done for your current or last employer?" You become respected based on the outcome that you have generated over the term of your employment. The idea is to always have income be the outcome of whatever it is that we do. This income could be knowledge but know that all income should be entering your life with a sign of respect.

Over the past decade, I started my career as a sales engineer and as an independent business owner. I can tell you that I have experienced both, and even though at times they were intimidating, I managed to pull through. I offered everyone respect in the beginning when I joined a company or when I was doing business. That said, respect then switched into an honor roll the moment I began taking on projects or delivering my product to clients.

If you're intimidated by the duties of the corporate world or the responsibilities of starting your own business, know you are not alone. Take control of your feelings and check yourself. Know that there are many out there, including this author, that are just like you, that face the same fears. Taking control of your career or business really starts, in my opinion, with honoring your word while respecting who's in front of you.

Have you watched *The Godfather* series? If not, you must. This series dictates the essence of respect and how to take control of situations to help benefit you and those around you. When the Godfather comes to those who are not on his level but approaches all with respect, he gains not only the respect of others but their loyalty as well. When we approach situations with that type of control, we then tend to turn the conversation to our benefit.

Do not think for a second that controlling your emotions and offering respect will have people talking positively about you. You will always have people who have nothing better to do than talk negatively of your name. Control your loyalty to your word and stay quiet. At times, you learn about what is being said to you behind your back, good or bad; learn to stay quiet and observe. Do not approach, do not confront, but rather learn and hold tight. Do not even offer disrespect, because the most brutal of weapons is good treatment toward those who betray you.

Exit Thoughts

Reflecting back on this chapter I have realized that I can keep writing for days about what it is that makes a difference in control. Maybe it is best that I keep it short and sweet. It started with me asking how control is defined. I started defining it through the five fingers of control. I always thought it wouldn't be easy writing this chapter as it included so much more than just my experiences.

I truly believe that respect, honor, and loyalty are embedded within us. If we learn to control the respect we give others, we can begin to live a more fulfilling life. Thinking back, I know there were a few people who didn't deserve my respect, and I may have overextended my hand. Reflecting now a few years later, I wouldn't change a thing. I realize that people may have their own image and story about me, but one common theme is the respect I always gave. I was able to control who I gave my respect to. At times, I stopped allowing those people to disrespect me by simply not acknowledging their respect. I guess when people get the same treatment they give off, they notice their wrongdoing.

Allow yourself to move past situations that no longer serve you. Create your own world and place that match your standards at a level that you are okay with. Control your being and what you want in your life in order to become great.

I liked this chapter, and I gave you my all through the text. I am satisfied with the content, and I hope it gives you a different point of view when it comes to control.

CHAPTER 7

The Emergency Button

Take a breather and simply stop. It isn't all that serious, it really isn't. If you think I am talking about life, you are wrong. I am talking about the difficult situation you are currently in, whatever it is. I know you'll hear people say that it's only a phase and that you'll get out of it; or they'll try to downplay it, like it doesn't cause you a mountain of stress and mental anxiety. But **stop** and **breathe**.

This too will blow over, and when it does, it will give you an idea of what you can or cannot do. Just don't mess up again. It isn't something that lasts long. You know what does? Death. Even then, you leave with no problems, and you leave it all behind.

I have been through so much, and I guarantee you have as well. You are going through your own big or little problem that has amounted to you stressing yourself. But here's the good news: it's not worth it, really. You will hear me say this over and over and over again: ***it is not worth it!***

I thought I would leave my troubles in 2018, but here I am in 2020, and I'm facing a whole new book of problems that life has thrown at me, and I did not even plan for this. I didn't think I would make the move I made in May 2019 with my job, but I did. It was months and months since I was last happy at my job, and I was doing absolutely nothing about it. I had deteriorated in a way that had me lost in a world that I was once able to navigate blindly. I did not know my way, and my moral compass was confused by its direction. Not having any other plan or back up, I was faced with either staying and slowly giving myself away or getting up and leaving.

I had written my resignation letter in March, in hopes that I would find another job before leaving, but that wasn't the case. I stayed and had the conversations with management about what was happening and what needed to happen; however, nothing changed. April passed, and then came May, and I was still in the same rut. So often during the day my colleagues would belittle me, and I wanted to blow my lid, but I didn't, as I knew I had to take a breather and simply **stop**. I had to stop my mind from thinking negatively and allowing people to control its state.

May came, and I had a conversation with someone at the company, and then I had a total breakdown. I was pushed so far that I, a grown man, was breaking down over a job that paid me so little and was literally destroying me. I was told, when the phone call was done, that I needed to take a breather and not quit. I took a breather, I stopped dead in my tracks, and I evaluated the situation. Within 15 minutes of getting off that phone call, I sat both my parents down and let them know I was resigning from my position.

That Sunday, I went up to the office and cleaned it out entirely. I had made up my mind that it was time I put a stop to this, so that I could regain control of my life. I had some savings on the side, enough to get me by for a little while, however it wasn't much. I knew that in order for me to advance as a human being, I would need to leave the company and go elsewhere.

Monday morning came, and it was May 13, 2019. At 8:30 a.m., I hit send on an email I had written on Sunday. During my stay at the office, while I was cleaning it out, I had an "aha" moment. I sat on my desk and reflected on all that I had done in the past 4 years, and I knew I was walking away with my head held high. I was happy and relieved that I was walking away from something that no longer served me. It felt amazing to be in control again, something that I had lost because of the toxic culture. Once I hit the "send" button, I took a breather and stopped. This time it was me thinking of what I need to do next and knowing that I had just rid myself of all the nonsense.

Mentally check out.

I was gone by the time they received my resignation letter (mentally checked out, that is). I felt so relieved and happy, and something told me that it would work itself out. I let it be, and I left and began my search only to find that there were so many more opportunities out there for me that paid so much more and had better work cultures. The moral of this incident is that even when it all hits the fan, you still have control of your life. Stop and smell the roses, for this life that we live is but one.

Was I worried that it wasn't going to work out? Sure. I was worried that my bills weren't going to be paid on time and that I was not bringing in any money or funds to help me sustain the life that I wanted. I couldn't do much about it, but I wasn't going to live the life of a sheep and not the one I wanted. For what is life if it is not one that you mold and shape into what you want?

Stop, breathe, and go. Take that step and believe in what you have to offer this world. You are born into it, and what you do while you are here is what will determine your happiness and your fate in the human race. Stop and breathe when it comes to a big offer you are getting or a huge step you are taking in life. It isn't the end of the world if you make the right or wrong one.

If you are afraid of what can be or what the future may hold for you, I need you to stop. Hit the emergency button if you have to and reset your mind to allow yourself to come to terms with the fact that the future is forgiving. What we cannot have today does not indicate what we can or can't have tomorrow.

Your mental health is most important and shouldn't be undervalued. In order for you to conclude when you need to hit the emergency button, you need to be mentally healthy. Know that if you keep your body in shape, your mind follows.

This is written out of frustration and anger, as I had to recently hit the emergency button. I had to place a stop to something that was hurting me more than it was helping me. This situation caused me all sorts of anxiety, depression, and stress, and it was because I couldn't control the situation amongst other things. Placing something in stop mode when it is spiraling out of control is difficult but not impossible. When my mind began overthinking all the outcomes, only one made sense. I couldn't continue on with uncertainty or with someone who wasn't able to place me first after I placed them in the forefront of my life for such a long time. I had stopped my life before to begin a new life with someone, and it proved to be an amazing experience. But maybe the experience was meant to be stopped or halted reaching a destination. I knew that this stop wasn't permanent, and if it was meant to be, it would pick up where we left off.

Life is similar to a car: you stop and go.

When was the last time you were able to walk? And when I say walk, I mean truly walk the earth we are all born into. Walk and observe your surroundings and place everything in stop mode. Let the sand creep up between your toes while you walk on the beach or let your hair down while the wind blows through it. Allow your life to stop for a few minutes and regain consciousness of the moment. We allow life to go past us at such a fast rate that we tend to forget to STOP and appreciate our blessings.

I say this because it happened to me. Even though I got myself out of multiple rat race events in my life, I somehow tended to find myself back in one. I am currently removing myself from the rat race and learning once again to live in the moment. I am stopping my mind from racing and my heart from aching while learning to walk again.

I had the good fortune of falling in love recently, a love that is timeless struck me and will forever be embedded within the deepest cells of my body. This type of love would occupy your day by the mere thoughts of future happiness, dances in the sun, and sleepless nights under the stars. A love that had placed my mistrust in society and love itself on hold. I didn't think for a second that it would be possible, but I did the moment my heart trusted another. This is exactly when I saw colors again, and the hatred I had in me stopped. I am forever grateful for that love and for the experience that my heart was able to go through. I had gone from machine to human, and I was able to feel, touch, see, and be again.

With my brother's passing, my trust in humanity diminished. I never wanted to get attached to anyone, as I knew there would be a chance that I could lose them. My attachment issues as a kid popped back up when I was an adult, so when I found this love, my heart was full. I was already happy, but my heart had endured a loss from a few years before that I simply did not want to handle again. Now that I have given you this description of my love to this person, let me tell you why I had to relax and take a breather.

I previously spoke about what brought me to the point of extinction with my previous employer and how the mental anxiety brought me to quit and start a new page. See, nothing in life is perfect, and nothing really comes with the whole package. We are led to believe that love isn't enough, but in reality, it is. Take a look at the older generation that only had love. They persevered through it all and made it work ... they had no other option. Love is still enough, as love will make you do things you never thought possible and reach levels of a full heart that you may never have thought you had. It's teamwork to say the least. Now with the love I had experienced, I took it from the start as a serious commitment and one that I was not to play with. I knew from the get-go that I was not going to be indecisive and would communicate all my passions and feelings. Almost 2 years later, it came to a pause and an end.

A human being can only endure so much until the limit is reached. Although I had given all that I could to the woman I was with, it somehow wasn't enough to continue. Now, is that a bad thing? No, not at all. I am not saying I am not enough, but rather that maybe the relationship wasn't where it needed to be.

Sometimes you encounter right human wrong timing and feel that "this could have been it." Don't think for a second that you yourself aren't enough for your significant other. Even though I am only speaking from my end, I can safely say that there was the same amount of love and effort given from her side as well. I had more than 2 years of successfully giving this woman everything one would desire from their significant other; however, we came to a point where outside circumstances dictated our fate.

Now although promises are meant to be kept, this one wasn't. Circumstances had surrounded us, and the decision to stay and build in the same city I was in was always up in the air, and opinions about things we discussed always changed. This in no way makes anyone a bad human being or a bad partner, not in the slightest. She is one of the sincerest, most innocent, and most beautiful human beings I have encountered in my life, and she was able to bring love into my life. a gift I can never repay.

But here's the thing: how much more can one endure? At the beginning of 2021, a new topic came up, and she expressed her concerns once again, and this time, we were not sure if we were ever going to be in the same country again. This is where I had to STOP everything.

I had to step up the game, add fuel to the fire, set the fire ... I had to do something before I caught myself losing me again. I learnt from my mistakes in the past and didn't want to end up where I was again in 2019. When the topics that were causing me anxiety and leading to no actual commitment came back up around New Year of 2021, and I had to decide. This is when I placed a pause to the relationship.

It is hard to walk away from love when there are no factors that lead to hatred but rather circumstances. I had placed all my effort, mental strength, capabilities, and all that I had into this relationship, because I believed in our love and our future together, even more importantly. I knew my girl did, too, and that's why I kept going.

I knew I was able to pause because of one incident a few days prior. I had washed my face, looked up, and realized that I saw a reflection of my brother looking back at me, similar to Simba and Mufasa, as cringy as that may sound. When I saw my brother's reflection, I realized that my biggest loss in life was looking back at me.

Once you endure the pain of death, yet you still are alive, nothing can come close to hurting you. You don't have to feel the pain I felt to come to that realization, and you can have your own type of pain too. It wasn't easy, what we did, and I am still struggling with it. I had to let go of my forever love because she wasn't ready for me or for us, and that's okay. Regardless of the reasons that she or I had, I had to come to terms with that. I had to take a breather, a step back, and say to myself, "What is it that actually matters that will warrant my mental health?" I had to figure this out on my own.

Throughout the relationship, I had committed to never walking away from her, yet I had always given her the ability to distinguish between a life with me or without me. Meeting halfway and compromise are truly what relationships that work are structured on. There may be times when you take those extra few steps and know that, as long as it's in the name of love, it's acceptable. Things had taken their toll on us, however, and I believe at one point we were both being dragged down by the circumstances. I became to believe that if we were meant to be, destiny would have us find our way back to each other, as I know that the love we had was the realest we'd experienced.

Before you judge her, know she had admitted all of this, but I had chosen to stay in it because of my fear of losing her. This was partially my way of keeping my feelings under control, as I didn't want her for the short-term but for the long-term. In the great words of Kenny Rogers, "Know when to fold 'em; know when to walk away." This was my emergency button, my stop to all things that were toxic to both of us. It wasn't fair that I was up in limbo, and it wasn't fair that she was with someone who was constantly anxious and dealing with unhealed trauma.

The emergency button is definitely a metaphor for stopping and regaining consciousness. This snap back into reality, into the real you, does more good than harm. With anxiety and our everyday problems, we are constantly facing a 'stop-and-go mentality' with every decision we make. Some decisions weigh heavier than others, but that's okay. You don't need to evaluate the weight of each decision. I in no way mean that this should result in an irrational decision-making lifestyle, but rather one where you're not taking on the stress associated with it. In these instances, I ask that you STOP, take a breather ... then relax and come back to the situation that requires a decision.

You are not defined by time.

Please know that you are not defined by what needs to happen now or by the consequences. Although you are running in a rat race of a life, you are living and alive, and that is more valuable than any type of stress that you can encounter. If you are not living in a rat race and already believe in this concept, then I am happy that we are on the same page. If you are stressing because you are not where you want to be in life, stop and breathe. If you are stressing about your friends surpassing you at an earlier stage in their lives, stop and breathe.

We all have different lives that encompass so much more than a race. My life hasn't been one that was in any way normal or one that was your typical 'Canadian upbringing.' From moving around multiple times to starting over from scratch, to losing my brother, I was always starting over. There were multiple times where I thought that my friends had surpassed me and moved beyond my success, but I quickly realized that I needed to stop this comparison. My circle was tight, and I knew I was surrounded by successful individuals who had their own battles and upbringings that caused them their own stress and anxiety. We all have stories that make us beautifully human. (If you don't know what I'm talking about, go back and reread Chapter 2.) Knowing that my path in life had been delayed due to circumstances, I knew that it was okay, but I wouldn't let it define me.

You are not defined by your circumstances or what happened to get you to where you are. You must realize that you shouldn't stress about all the problems that happened to you or weigh those heavily in your life. You must, however, take action to change your current position and get to a better place. My brother's passing had changed the course of my life forever, and it had taken me to a new place with new people and a new life. While my friends continued their lives, mine was uprooted within less than 24 hours. During the period when I left the country and started a new life in Lebanon, I found that I had to tell myself to stop and breathe. I was too concerned with stressing myself out about where I needed to be rather than where I was. I figured that I had to set my goals for writing in the future and work on them in the meantime.

Don't be fooled by what you see on social media. It's social for a reason and gives you a false imprisonment of what you should be, which defaults you to stress and anxiety. I can't teach you how to displace that or let it go, but rather I can tell you what I have done. Social media will have you thinking that you are so far behind in life, that you are constantly in GO mode, that you have no reason to stop, you have no reason to slow down; that's exactly what social media does to you. Regardless of what platform you are using, people post what they want you to see rather than what is. If you really think about it, you will find this exact statement to be true, and you yourself will know what a lie everyone is living.

Vulnerability takes a special type of human being. Do not be gullible enough to believe what you see, thinking it is the new norm, because it isn't. I have been a victim and perpetrator in this as well. I have placed pictures and quotes on my social platforms that would make people think I am living a life of bliss; meanwhile, I am slowly dying on the inside.

You are the reader of your life, and you need to read between the lines on what it is you are interpreting. You need to stop and refocus your energy on your life and what defines you. Please do not give in to these posts or images or words that are given out so easily. If you find yourself in this spiral, where you are lingering and waiting to clench onto something powerful on social media, STOP and lock yourself out for a little while. You need to reconnect with your truest self before you continue on with your days. In these instances, it isn't best that you start a friendship or relationship until you are ready to start one with yourself.

A friend once told me that the 4 pillars that you will need for true alignment are physical, mental, spiritual, and emotional. I truly believe that in order to stop the emergence of harmful toxins within your life, you must attempt to merge all four in unison. If you find somehow that one is out of balance with the others, you must attempt to stop this teeter totter of the pillars. You may not be able to really find the reason behind why all that is happening, but that really isn't for you to overthink.

If there are situations that affect your physical being in a way that erodes your health, know that your mind follows suit. The days of growing old while neglecting your mental health issues are over. We are continuously developing into a society of influencers that have control over our emotions on a minute-by-minute basis. Once your body declines you need to stop whatever is causing this and snap out of it.

I noticed this pattern in myself multiple times over during 2020. My anxiety would be at an all-time high, and I would eat for comfort. This eating habit then disabled any mental strength that I had, and my spirituality followed shortly. I really didn't notice my fix for my anxiety until the beginning of 2021, where I caught myself having an anxiety attack, and my first go-to was food. Don't be surprised. I am writing to you as a human being and a student of life. Even though I had started working on my physical self and had stopped my bad eating, I noticed that one exception when I was losing control.

I had started to regain my health after months of letting loose and not stopping the downward spiral of depression and anxiety in 2020. Even though my body was regaining its appearance and my health was improving, my mental side was still the aspect I had to fix. I realized that I needed to stop all that was affecting and creating these effects. I was in such a constant battle to be great and make as much money I could that I didn't realize my spirit was off. Anything that I wanted to manifest wasn't for the long run, but for the short run, and the manifestation was convoluted by toxins that I didn't see.

Most of the time we humans want what we can have now, yet we forget that anything you can build takes time. The race to be great was affecting me in a way that I couldn't have believed, and really, I didn't see the man I was becoming until I became the man I didn't want to be. I couldn't figure out why nothing was working in my favor... was it because I was so lost in my purpose? Was it because I was not aware of the long-term goals I had to set? Was it because I was afraid of loss once again? Everything led to me telling myself I need to STOP and smell the flowers.

At times you will find yourself in a train of emotions, rules, events, and practices that are just not what you should be riding. It's okay to fall back every once in a while; we are human. But remember that it is you who can place a STOP to this, and that you can regain your truest self. I stopped rushing things, stopped moving so quickly, and stopped pushing and reacting to situations that did not warrant my immediate emotions. I had to let life be. I had to stop my toxic way of beating myself up for not being where I wanted to be in my life. The moment you allow yourself to be yourself in the present moment you will become the person you want to be tomorrow.

A very good friend of mine, who was going through a divorce and other issues that could destroy someone, said, "It's okay, I'll be fine. I'm alive now and will continue to remain alive as long as I am living in this moment." I later asked him what he meant (after he regained a normal life) and his answer was so simple. He indicated that he had to put a stop to what had defined him in the past. As long as he was living in the present moment, with an understanding that any plan for the future may change, he was alive and well.

Now that is a healthy way of thinking, and here's why: most of us forget to live in the moment, to be alive in the now, and I think that's where we go wrong. The majority of us, rather the majority of those I know, are living, yet they are so wrapped up with stress and confusion of the future that they forget the now. The long-term goals that you associate with your capabilities are only going to be reached if you focus on today. Focus on your goals for this day.

This is where your 4 pillars of success come into play. You see, once your physical health is on point, and your mental health is being rehabilitated, your emotions fall in line. The ability to stop your immediate reaction to a situation, calm down, gather your emotions, and regain mental cognizance means that you have won. As I mentioned before, not every situation needs an immediate reaction, and I promise you this will only happen once your physical self takes a healthy turn. When your physical, mental, and now emotional pillars align themselves, your spirituality automatically comes next.

See we are only here on earth for a limited time; however, our spirits may exist for eternity. This is and will always be the case. Depending on what type of legacy you want to leave behind, your spirituality can be defined in any aspect, from religion, to belief in God, to whatever it is you choose.

What worked for me was that I had to stop my bad habits cold turkey, to literally shock my system so that I could adapt to new habits. I think my biggest obstacle to overcome is my mental ability to accept what happened on January 24, 2011. Most of my depression, flashbacks, and current day societal distrust stem from that day. Usually, if my mental self is off, my physical tends to decline as well.

I remember having a conversation with my father—who, by the way, is one of the smartest men I know—about mental exhaustion. I told him that if the mind is overworking and exhausted, my body finds itself in a state of fatigue as well. My emotions flutter, and my spirit becomes off as well. He looked at me and said, "You're so right, that's the truth." And if there was anyone in the world who could agree with me, it was him, and that was really all I needed to hear to get back on my feet. I needed to stop the entry of these negative thoughts immediately and start forcing my body into an active mode. I was sitting in front of a man, my father, who really had a hard,

hard life. I mean, I don't know how he is still alive; the circumstances of his life alone would destroy me.

My father was an engineer in his earlier days and a successful one to say the least. When he married my mother, he knew he had to find a better life in Canada, and his trip to immigrate here wasn't easy. From leaving my mother and I only 10 days after I was born, to claiming asylum in Sweden, to hiding in a bathroom until his plane took off, the man has been through it. I am not mentioning the multiple times where life would kick in, and he would have to work long hours so that his family could have something to eat. I think the hardest thing he has endured is the loss of his son, my brother. So, when he said that to me, I thought that if someone of his caliber can say so and move past it, why was I being so weak?

Sometimes if you're looking for strength, regardless of what pillar you need, it could be as close as a parent for you to hold on to. After looking him in the eye, I walked away ashamed that I had let small situations get to me. That was another incident when I had to stop, relax, and take in my surroundings so that I could get up and build for tomorrow.

The foundation of tomorrow is the essence of today.

If 2020 was any sort of indication, it was to STOP and smell the flowers. I think it's safe to say that our grandkids will probably hear about the year that placed a global STOP on the world. That year humbled a lot of people and allowed all of us to realize that even if the world economy were to stop, it wouldn't be the end. Now, of course, it did take a hit. I think we all did, but we continued our lives. In my opinion, the silver lining with the pandemic is that we were all forced to stop our lives and start living again. I know I started spending time with my family and started to learn new attributes about them all.

Was it healthy in the long run? NOPE. The pandemic introduced a concept to the free human race that it isn't used to being imprisoned. We became captives of this virus that really did strip us of our daily conveniences. Let's face it, we are all spoiled in some aspects of our lives. There are people who have it much worse than we do, and yet we always complain. Pre-pandemic, we had become a race of individuals who were pre-occupied by greed. I have personally seen this pandemic humble a lot of individuals who now recognize the good in doing deeds and helping others. What stopped during the pandemic became the go ahead for a lot more.

Yet the lockdowns were not healthy in the long run. I even became a victim of depression and stress all over again because I couldn't do my simplest of tasks. When humanity is stripped of its essentials, chaos ensues. This chaos doesn't necessarily need to be by the masses for the masses, but rather it might be mental and spiritual chaos. Seeing that everything was stopped forced a lot of us outside with friends and family.

As much as a plus as this was, it was tough for a lot of us during the winter. One of the toughest times occurred when I was home alone and the quiet hit. You somehow know that you are limited to what you can do, and even though social media has you connected with the world, you still feel disconnected. I found myself once again deteriorating physically, which was leading to my mental, emotional, and spiritual disintegration as well.

I was placed in yet another corner when my previous love and I broke up, and I was fending away this loneliness. I started really feeling the quietness in my home. I realized that I needed to think outside the box about what it was I could do or feel at that very moment to maintain sanity. One of the things that worked for me was my surroundings, and here's how: I started looking at different things that needed to get done around the house, and I told myself that in order to conquer my anxiety or loneliness, I needed to feel accomplished. I made a list of all the small things that needed fixing, and I started. They really ranged from housework to getting groceries. One by one, I completed the tasks. What I'm really trying to say is that I wasn't putting aside my feelings of anxiety and frustration, but I was stopping these emotions by keeping myself busy with tasks that were accomplishments.

These were only tasks that I could look at as a reminder of something I was able to finish. I managed to somehow create new workouts at home and to define my physical ability once again and this was a major help. I am not boasting but rather letting you know what I did during this WORLD STOP that got me out of my rut, in hopes that you may have done the same thing or rather can do the same thing. Getting into the different aspects that got me out of my rut could help you, and that really is the whole goal of this book.

I guess we really need to stop and relax through different points of our lives. Though we may have different definitions of "relax," I think the most important one is that we remain *healthy.* The shedding of these toxins, whether they are spiritually, emotionally, physically, or mentally, is always an important task. I learned a lot through the 2020 era or "a disaster of a year" as some like to call it.

Learn yourself, really learn what makes you tick. Learn how the art of saying no to yourself and disciplining your emotions when it comes to the aspects of your life that you feel are important to you. Believe me when I tell you, no one will care for your health as much as you will, and that is why it is important you find the inner beast in you and continuously choose what is best for you. I believe that we all have the ability to do so, and it is within us as humans to choose. The gift of choice is the best gift of all. Choose wisely and remember to continuously keep your 4 pillars aligned.

Exit Thoughts

This chapter was really a mix up of so many emotions and thoughts. I have tried to convey the thought of the word STOP and its theory—my theory, at least. There were a lot of individuals and aspects of my life within the last 10 years that really contributed this chapter, and I have to give each person their due. There are a lot of instances in your life that may have changed who you are today, and I promise you that is okay. Who you are today is a human being who is so unique that you really cannot exist anywhere else. Your life and what has happened in your life has made you one of one (even if you're a twin).

I have been affected by a lot of people and their actions, and I always try to reflect on how I got out of each circumstance. I usually spend 10 to 15 minutes at night thinking about how I could have gone about the situation and what I learnt from it. Some situations I can't really do much about other than to try and accept them.

My brother's passing wasn't and still isn't a situation that I have accepted. The impact it has had on my life makes it the only circumstance that I have yet to learn how to put a stop to, including the toxic thoughts stemming from that night. I may temporarily stop it, but I have yet to learn how, and that is fine. I am as you are, a student of life on this journey, learning how to become great, and I accept that. I am alive today, and I won't stop living as I have multiple reasons to stay alive.

If you need motivation or a reason to push through, look at someone close to you who you know has been through it. Whether it is your parents, friends, or family, reflect on what they went through and then attempt to find the silver lining in

145

what you are going through today. Being grateful will never be out of fashion.

Stay safe, and always—I repeat, always—stop and smell the flowers.

CHAPTER 8

Can You Hear Me?

C an you hear yourself? Is it possible that you aren't listening to yourself? Listen. I mean it. Listen to understand. Most of us don't do that but rather listen and try to formulate a response prior to the end of the argument.

Can you hear the way you are speaking? What words are spewing out of your mouth and into the world that become your vibe? Did you ever think about not using some of the words that come to mind, but rather replacing them with more positive and reassuring ones?

Sometimes we exhaust ourselves with the fact that we don't give ourselves credit when it comes to who we are. Some of us seemingly joke around about our own traits, not realizing that these words eventually become the reality that we don't want. When some people speak about how they cannot do something, they've already psyched themselves out on that subject. I have been there. I have stopped myself mid-sentence because I caught myself saying things that I did not want to become my reality.

That is what this chapter is about: **communication.** Whether it is with your loved one, people, work, career, goals, or more importantly, yourself. Understanding that what we say has a larger impact on the receiving end than we realize is a key aspect here.

I want to take you through the last ten years of my life and how communication was incorporated. I want you to realize that some of my stories may be relatable and so authentic that you may feel something towards my words. I have been able to experience all the different rates of communication thrown my way on two different continents. I never really started off as this guy who communicated his feelings or even his thoughts. It really did take me losing everything twice, and then finding it again (and then some), to realize that communication is the key to it all. I wanted people to hear me, but I soon realized, I couldn't hear myself. I was shouting at the wrong crowd about how I wanted to feel and to be treated by them. I wanted control of opinions and subjective minds even though my mind was the least controlled. I wasn't communicating with myself at all, and through that journey, I was able to learn that the basis of our life itself is communicating.

Can you hear me? Yes, you in the mirror!

Before 2011, I was living a fast-paced life, an entrepreneurial one to say the least. I was up at 6 a.m., worked until 2 p.m., and was back in my office by 4 p.m., working on a social engineering site that I had started with my best friend. I would not get out of my chair unless it involved making a quick flip of some type of product. I was still hustling on the side when it came to the financing. I would pick up small quantities of clothing or electronics and make the flips during the week. I could easily make $1,000 during the week, in cash. I would then usually see my girlfriend in the evening and top it off by going to sleep at 11 p.m. This was my fast-paced life, but in the midst of it all was one thing: the communication I had with myself.

There wasn't a time that I said I couldn't do anything. I knew for a fact at that time that it was best I thought of myself as a beast, an untamable human being capable of doing anything he wants. If there was a certain type of business I wanted to get into, I would find a way to build it and push it forward. During these times I was able to push this mentality onto others.

I remember I would sit there and watch videos of people who got excited every time they accomplished a major feat in their life. There was one video that I still watch till this day, a video of P. Diddy jumping out of his chair after he closed a deal and saying that he can't be stopped. This is the energy that I used to place out there for myself that I communicated with myself.

Then 2011 happened.

After the night when my brother passed away in my arms, along with everything else of my life, I was able to question every single move that crossed my mind. Not only was my trust in society gone, but my communication with myself was also nonexistent. It was like all the self-confidence I had built for myself had simply vanished. After that night, I moved from house to house in an attempt to stay secure and low-key. Here I was, a man who always stood up in front of people now in hiding. This killed my self-confidence in ways that I never thought possible.

In times of distress, you should always try to stay level-headed. Attempt to stay true to your beliefs without being drowned by the outside noise. If you by any means shy away from your ability to believe that only what you see is true, you will fall to those doubters around you. The naysayers, the beings who are destroying your communication with yourself. Remember that when everything hits the fan, only the strong survive. Push yourself to stay mentally strong. This is where communication plays such a pivotal role in your ability to come out on top.

Following the days of my brothers passing, there was a tornado of rumors that started hitting our area. We heard everything from, "His brother set him up," to "He was involved in so much other stuff." The list went on. This had me fueled with anger, because I knew the truth, but it was so hard hearing the public think so negatively about me. I didn't know it at the time, but I believe this is when my anxiety started introducing itself into my life. From then on, I would question my every decision, because it was implanted in my head to do so. If you're wondering, here's how: I would go from meeting to meeting, police station to offices, to recap everything I had seen that night. The one question that kept coming up was, "Are you sure?" This caused me to question myself and my character. After that, my anxiety led me to question every situation I was ever in.

Mind you, I was broken. I had just lost my brother, and all I kept thinking about was the moment I ran to him with my father, grabbed him, and saw him. My confidence stopped, and my communication with myself stopped. This was the beginning of my downfall.

I would question myself about whether or not I was able to remember the specific details. Not sure of how to act, my confidence in myself deteriorated quickly. I no longer thought of myself as an unstoppable force but rather as a human being susceptible to anyone and everyone around me. What was it that I could say to myself that would boost my confidence? There was actually nothing, in reality, that could.

After approximately 14 days, we left Canada. When we got to Lebanon, I was now more confused than ever. Not knowing how to gain control over my life, or rather who I was, I was placed in a city where I knew nobody. Heck, I didn't even know the rules of the country yet. I was introduced to family members that I had never seen before, who attempted to control me and my actions. I was so weak that when I would be out, I would simply start randomly crying, remembering my brother. Till this day, it angers me to remember how fragile I had become.

Basically, not knowing who I was or how I was going to move forward, I decided to stay quiet with my communication. This helped but hurt me, and people were always in my business. Society by nature is nosey, and people want to know what's going on and need the drop on the latest news.

Let's open up a bit.

I decided to open up about what happened to 3 of my friends, and boy, did I regret it. When I opened up, I realized 2 things: I was communicating my pain to people who didn't care, but rather wanted to be the first to hear it. The fact is that I felt stupid, as I barely heard from them. This instigated my self-doubt, and I immediately began to regret my decision. Was it the right one? Why was I opening up to people when I couldn't even look at myself in the mirror? After a year or so, I really began to develop my confidence again. After the dust settled, I realized that I needed to put out the energy that would help me rebuild. I started shelling out emotions that didn't serve me, opinions that had no immediate effect, and, more importantly, people.

Can you hear me?

I started hearing myself again. Every time I would speak, I would imagine myself standing across from myself, wondering how what I said was interpreted. This gave me a perspective on myself that I had never seen before. I was a baby learning how to crawl and walk again. The moment I realized that the words I speak about myself are more than projections, but rather actual physical manifestations, everything changed.

Did you ever hear the phrase "the moment you start thinking positive, positive things will happen?" Start speaking positively and see what happens. It'll knock your socks off. The moment you start developing a new vocabulary of synonymic

"I can's," your view really does change. Try cussing less. Saying things like "I'm stressed," or "There's no hope," will have you stressed with no hope. Now I'm sure, that isn't an image of yourself that you want.

Let's face it: no one wants to be in the slums and have weak confidence. We all attempt to make it to the top with the confidence we require. Most just fail to realize that the ability to start projecting self-confidence is only a step away. What we speak into existence will slowly become our aura. The vibe we place out there starts with the words that seep off your tongue. Why do you think romance is the way it is? It's not because of an intangible feeling that you somehow come across, but rather you speak sweet words of love that slip off the tongue into the heart of the receiver. When a man wants to sweet-talk his woman, he will place the right words together to make sure he is communicating the love, so that she can feel the energy.

Imagine if you did that with yourself, that you spoke positive reinforcement to yourself. You can even sweet talk yourself into self-love. You stand there and develop a loving appreciation for who you are, where you have been, and where you are bound to go. You speak to yourself in a loving manner and acclimate to this newfound aura. Having a small dip where your confidence shifts is okay too. Remember Chapter 2, that as you are, you are beautiful. I spoke about this exact situation, when your energy shifts a little, but you are content because you are a human being.

Do you hear yourself? Seriously, the next time you are out there in public, look at your surroundings and attempt a better reading of yourself. Don't become self-conscious (God, no). This isn't the tale of questioning your every move, but rather the story of becoming a better communicator with yourself. Adapting your mind to speak positive reinforcements with yourself is such a beautiful thing to do.

Are you capable of speaking with yourself the way you want to speak to others? Imagine someone spoke to you the way you spoke to them; would that be it? I will get into communication with other people; however, it starts with you, the reader. Back to the story at hand now and how communication ties into it.

I ended up leaving Lebanon only to come back to Toronto, to a whole new world again. I wasn't the same person. The smallest shred of confidence that I had built up by communicating with myself was now gone. I remember walking around with a hoodie, a hat, and sunglasses, because I wasn't okay with people knowing where I was. I was worried at the time, because the individuals that caused my brother harm were still out there. I would walk with my head low, and I wouldn't be too happy about things.

The amount of confidence that can come from just raising your head is mind-boggling, and I slowly began coming out of my shell. I started implementing the same process that I had in Lebanon back in Toronto. I started speaking in much softer tones and forgiving myself for things that were out of my control. I started allowing my mind the acceptance of understanding more than anything.

To create your aura, you must give understanding a chance. The ability to forgive your mistake because you didn't know better will always place you ahead of the race. Once in Toronto I started developing a life where relationships would start again, and new faces would enter my life. I started realizing that communication was much further than just speaking with myself in the right tone.

To whom am I speaking?

Allow reality to hit you every once in a while, or take advantage of the situation and face it immediately. We promote and sell ourselves on a daily basis, and one of the main acts of self-promotion is communication. We either communicate properly and don't sell our selves short or vice versa. The generation that now exists really has united all different ages into one, dependent, non-communicative race. We have more options, which allow us to always be open to new opportunities, which leads to less communication. So much can be lost in translation if communication isn't utilized properly. What Sally says about Jennifer can be lost in translation by the time the message makes it to Mike.

Most of us enter into each other's lives with a notion that in time we will build a relationship together. This can only be on a solid foundation if both individuals are willing to explicitly communicate their feelings, emotions, and standards. You as a human being must, in all vulnerability, learn to express your thoughts to the audience in front of you so that you can carry on healthy relationships.

I, like most of you, have gone through multiple relationships, some that lasted longer than others, were healthier than others, and some that were the total opposite. I have had lifelong friends become absent from my life because of misunderstandings and have had relationships end because of assumptions. We really do not give the word "communication" it's well-deserved definition in our lives. I have had friends hold grudges against me because of their misunderstanding, which would have been solved had we communicated correctly.

Now, I am not telling you to be an open book with the world, but rather to create a bond between those who matter to you by speaking your mind. If 2021 has taught us anything it's that it's time to start communicating with each other on a more honest and genuine level. Look around you, find who is most important to you, and think about how you can make that relationship better. I guarantee that you will find communication to be on your list of things to improve.

What holds value to you most when it comes to expressing your emotion or feelings? Is it your pride? Is it your ego? Is it that you may be scared that the person listening to you may not be empathetic? Or that they rather have ulterior motives as to why they are hearing you out? These are all valid questions and concerns that you may have as a human being and as one who is looking to improve their life. Realize that you aren't the only one in this boat. We're all sailing in the same ocean, just some in different directions.

Do you not understand what I'm saying?

When you realize that it is a topic of improvement you must realize that it's going to take some serious effort. Communication is going to take work and a budget of time but will give back 10-fold as an investment. The moment you realize that you are ready to improve your relationships with communication is the moment your life becomes great again.

Think about it. If you must, reflect. Reflect on the last argument that you had with someone close to you and how it played out. What would have happened if you had communicated differently, and not gotten mad, but rather thought about how the person across from you is understanding your words. Some of us speak our words as we understand them and not as the person in front of us is receiving them. People have emotions, and nowadays, emotions play a huge role with how the structure of a sentence is understood. When speaking, know that you may be misunderstood, and anger may arise from the context of the conversation.

Believe it or not, sometimes placing a period at the end of a sentence or word in a text message means you are firm or dry. This can affect someone's day because they aren't 100%. Now it is also up to that someone to communicate that they aren't having a good day, so that both individuals can be on the same page. This could literally mean absolutely nothing as well, and that's why it's important to understand your partner's communication.

Within us, in our minds and hearts, is storage space for a multitude of emotions. We can hold grudges against people, be upset with people, and become heartbroken, all while being quiet about it. I ask you this: why hold it in? Why not communicate this hurt and pain so that you can be at peace with yourself? I get that sometimes the person you are holding a grudge against hurt you, but you're hurting yourself by holding in all this pain. Why not speak to them about what is causing you grief? I can tell you why you wouldn't, because sometimes the person you want to speak to about your issue takes one side or rather is narrow-minded or is so selfish that they don't want to see how or what they have done to you. With that I say, "Move on." Let go. Attempt to communicate; however, if they aren't willing to understand you or make amends, you must let it be.

Communication with people is an art. People understand differently, and it really isn't something we can control. What we can control is the learning experience of how we set our communication amongst different people. We must learn each other's way of communicating, especially when it comes to friendships and relationships. In order to sustain a healthy relationship, you must observe and make notes of how everyone around you really is. This means that you need to spend time with people, and you must be vulnerable as well. We all may speak English, but we have our own languages. Whether it is the way we walk, talk, create hand gestures, or even when we are absolutely quiet, we have our own language. Think of your current or previous partner. What's their language like? Are they the type to show you love or speak love? Are they the type to show you they care by buying you gifts or rather catering to your needs? If you are willing to interpret their language, then you must experience their history. You can start by understanding where they have spent the last 10 or 15 years and how their upbringing has been. Most of us who have come to the U.S. or Canada come from immigrant families that understand love and communication in different ways.

Some individuals understand love by purchasing gifts and showering their friends or lovers with items. Some may even go above and beyond on normal occasions. I have friends who express their concern or love with words rather than actions and that is fine. The fine line between denial and acceptance is within your mind.

I remember my relationship that essentially didn't work out (not sure if we will have rekindled the relationship by the time this is published). One specific thing that I can state is that had communication been better, we could have been healthier. You see, I have always been one to communicate my feelings and emotions with my partner; however, sometimes I encountered speed bumps that placed so much on hold. So many of our days were gone to waste because of a lack of communication. Where small issues can be talked about in minutes and solved, they trailed on for days. I remember thinking only that if the ego or pride could be let go for just a second, we could get past this.

If one of the two partners has a flaw in their communication skills, the flaw will rub off on the other. One communication issue definitely rubbed off on me and left me wondering where I went wrong with my actions. I started somehow acting the same a few months down the road, and it really wasn't healthy. It wasn't until one day where I had to crack the egg and spill the beans on everything that was bothersome to me about communicating with her that she realized something was wrong. She had acquired some of my flaws as well and had also opened up to me about what bothered her. I had fallen into the same unhealthy trap as well, and it deteriorated the relationship. That was our love, though, so if it meant either of us had to step up to the plate, we did. I couldn't control her, though. I might only have told her what bothered me and vice versa.

When is communication most important?

You want a healthy love? Communicate. You want a better lifestyle? Communicate. You want a better family atmosphere? Communicate. By all means necessary always speak about what bothers you so that a level of understanding is created.

Your loved one is going to be the backbone to your life. It is so important that we allow ourselves the decency of love by communication. If you are feeling restless and unhappy, it is on you to allow your partner to know that. You realize that we as homos sapiens are not mind readers, right? You wouldn't want to feel alone or have someone else feel alone even though you share the same bed with them, right? You must allow your heart to speak and your mind to translate the words to gain the peace between you two. I touched base on language earlier and how we all have our own. Ever think about the language of love and how love could be one of the most powerful things on this earth? The feeling of happiness, completeness, stability, and excitement are all wrapped into one word: love.

I remember falling in love with my girl at the time, and let me tell you, I had some walls up; however, I profoundly recall the moment all these emotions took over, and I felt it all at the same time. I was walking by the casino in Niagara after we had left the Dragon Fly Club for a friend's bachelor party. I remember standing in that club, and all I could think about was how I didn't want to be anywhere but in her arms. How her words when spoken made me, as a man, want to finally sleep in peace in her arms. As I was walking, I stopped and allowed my heart to communicate with my mind, and the words came out. "I love her," I said to a friend walking ahead of me. He called me crazy, but he couldn't feel the language we had built together run through my veins. It was adrenaline, it was excitement, it was as if I had discovered my own unlimited drug. I had to express this, and I believe I had texted her that night or called her the following day, expressing this, only to find out that she had fallen in love as well. This was the heart communicating and the mind speaking what I couldn't.

Take the time to learn your friend's language. If that friend if your lover, learn their language. Learn what bothers them, what ticks them off, and more importantly what they're dealing with when they are silent. Most of us speak in silence, and although it may be difficult to really get it, it isn't impossible.

How do I psyche myself out of bad thoughts?

Part of facing reality is the ability to control your mind toward what you want it to deal with, which in essence is learning how to strengthen your communication with yourself. The past year (2020 through 2021) hasn't been a kind. I can tell you that I have lost so much within these years, so that not only was it a wasted year but involved some of my hardest losses, from my rental unit being destroyed to taking a financial business hit to my relationship loss. I even settled the case on the murderers in my brother's death, which marked 10 years since my brother left us.

You can tell that my mind during this year had dealt with so much. I was slowly slipping back into depression and thoughts that I had since let go. My mind started working extra hard to the point where my anxiety was at an all-time high, and I was making up scenarios in my head that didn't exist. Trust me when I say that I was not healthy. Through a few breakdowns and anxiety attacks, I began to realize that I might need to ask for some help. This led to my current path of recovery.

I am not holding back anything in this book, and I am laying it all out on the line for you to read, hear, and hopefully feel. I started feeling depressed for many reasons, reasons that included the fact that I was stagnant, and I hated that. Others were that I was not sure of the future anymore, and I hated the fact that I had started relationships that couldn't progress. This slippage caused not only a tightness in my life but in those around me. How was I going to get out of it?

At first, I started communicating all my problems with my significant other; however, I clearly learned that that wasn't the healthiest of options. As men, we tend to embody a 'protect and serve' mentality when we are with our significant other, from 'all issues foreign or domestic.' How was I doing that if I was expressing to her my depression and stress? I knew I needed to communicate the depression out of my life. With the advice I was given, I looked up therapists. I found one, and I decided to seek help. This wasn't the way I thought I would ever deal with my depression and unhealed trauma, but it was worth it.

I needed to get better, not only for myself, but for those around me too. Nobody wants to deal with a negative individual all the time, and people want positivity and healthy relationships. I knew that in order for me to start healthy relationships with people, I needed one with myself. This is where I started with expressing my feelings to myself first prior to anyone else.

I did this by visiting my brother. I started speaking to him while going through my ups and downs. Even though it was a tombstone that I was speaking with, I knew that in some way shape or form, I was communicating with the person who would listen and take it in. I would pray when I was there with him. I would pray that those around me experiencing my issues would be given enough patience that they wouldn't walk away from my life while I figured things out. I remember one day when my depression got so bad that I went to visit

Shadi, and while up there I admitted to him I was contemplating offing myself. I felt as if I was hurting too many people with the depression I was feeling. (I'll touch base on dealing with pain in the next chapter, but for now let's go on.)

Apart from learning what I was dealing with, I had to take in the fact that I had let 10 years of unresolved issues build up. I had allowed myself to not communicate my problems and simply ran away for 10 years thinking that I was handling it; I wasn't. Trauma showed up every day and in my every relationship. I began to reflect on my love life and how I had really reflected parts of my depression through it and to the people I shared time with. If you are reading this and are one of the individuals, I have crossed paths with who was affected in a negative way, I apologize.

If there was anything that I stumbled upon that helped me in a huge way, it was reflection. My depression stems back from when we were kids and the constant moving that we dealt with. I understand and I hope you feel my words when I say that my parents gave my brother and me a life they could have only imagined when they were kids. My dad really hustled his life away to give us everything he didn't have. It stemmed from January 24, 2011. I had really started building up so many walls, and in 2020, it all came crumbling down at the expense of my freedom and happiness.

My mentality had changed. I had learned acceptance. The ability to surpass your pride or ego to speak to someone you have never met in your life is one to be proud off. If you're having problems that are defined in any manner, I suggest speaking with someone professional who can help. I had put off therapy for so many years. I had stopped giving people too much information about myself and learnt that it is best that people only got what I wanted them to hear. I needed to keep so much to myself because I was becoming monochromic. I stopped hearing from people and was seeing people less. My relationships with my friends, let alone my love, were always full of tension. I realized that if this was the case in general, there was no way that it was them, but rather me. I was part of it, so I must've been the reason.

Sometimes we don't realize it, but the fire that is burning a hole in our lives, really, is a fire within us that needs to be tamed or put out. Find what is causing your internal fire (and not the sexual fire that everyone thinks I'm talking about), that fire that isn't letting you sleep at night. Communicate with your mind and soul about why you are not at ease. Please, I beg of you, life is too precious to waste not knowing or not becoming greater. Be real with yourself about why things aren't right. Reflect and communicate with your reflection if you have to as to why you got angry and didn't speak properly.

The words that roll off our tongue can dictate a relationship or a conversation. As my dad would say, "Think before you speak," and I have never thought of that to be so important until now. When you are full of anger, do not make decisions and watch the words that come out of your mouth. When you are happy, do not make promises as they sometimes can fall into only that moment. Be kind with the way you communicate the words from your brain to your lips. Tainted lips never kissed anything sweet. One thing I realized about myself that I needed to stop was my continuous cussing. At times I would find that it was unnecessary and simply an ugly trait of mine.

It is what it is.

Half the time it is things that we can change in our lives that make it better. Let's not lie to each other here—we all are okay with tarnishing some relationships, but the relationship with yourself? "Nah, that ain't it, Chief."

Cutting depression cold turkey isn't easy, and it sometimes can't be done. It isn't like smoking. What you can do is to not give up on yourself. Do not allow yourself to give up on others either, or if you must find a reason to get better, look around. When I say you must start with "communicating depression out of your life," I mean that in the most subjective way. I can only tell you what has worked with me, and it is up to you to either take that to the bank or invest it or simply dump it.

Look, the way I see that I can communicate depression out of my life is to find a way to make my mind think otherwise. For years I wore a rubber band around my left wrist. What I would do is that every time I started thinking negatively or would overthink, I'd stretch it and snap it. It would hurt every time I did that, but I was training myself. People would ask why I would do that in public, and I'd say, "Out of habit," and move on. I didn't want to give anyone the reason, because I wasn't sure of the results, and more importantly, I was worried they'd laugh at me.

I've seen that people don't understand and are quick to judge someone when they themselves do not understand the issues. It may take them time, but I'm thoroughly convinced that they eventually can. For instance, I started adopting this method again in 2020, and I remember my friend at the time asking why I was snapping, and I finally explained it. I had to communicate my method of healing so that they could understand what their friend was going through. I would literally snap out of it every time that rubber band hit my wrist, and slowly but surely, I would get out of my attacks. I found a way to communicate depression out of my life.

Another tactic I used that helped me was that the moment I realized I was getting in my slump, I would message those close to me (my mom and my girl at the time), saying that I am not feeling 100%, and I may be falling back into my bubble. This did wonders for everyone as it didn't leave anyone in the dark about what was going on.

When my depression hit, it hit hard. I would communicate with myself the most negative of thoughts, as I really was angry at the world in so many ways. I hated the way my life was playing out, and I would go from 100% healthy to 0% in only a day. I realized that I couldn't place my emotions and thoughts in anyone else's hands, other than an outsider obliged to help me get better, so I sought a therapist. I had communicated this with others and the response I got was surprisingly positive. I had to admit and communicate with myself that it was time I heal. I couldn't bear losing more people, and as you may now know, it was one thing I hated the most.

If you are wondering how to get help, Google it. I'm dead serious. The internet has all the answers that you may be looking for. I ended up searching for a therapist that specialized in trauma and relationships. I made an appointment and ended up going to see her, and I promise you, it changed my life. You cannot communicate your depression out of your life with your friends or your family. A lot of people are happy you have the problem, and some don't even care. That's just the reality of things.

Code of Silence

You shouldn't give people too much information because it is always great to work in silence and let the results speak loudly. A lot can go sideways once you start revealing your hand. Take for example, *The Godfather*, when Vito Corleone was discussing a deal and was interrupted by his son. To his son, it didn't mean much, but to his enemy, it meant the world. It swayed the deal in favor of his opponent, as he knew that Vito was the one stopping the situation from happening.

In 2020 and 2021, nothing much has changed about the ability of people holding something against you. I am revealing a lot, but I promise you, I leave some secrets to myself. I haven't revealed to anyone other than my mother and my girl at the time that I started seeing a therapist. Now whoever is reading knows.

As you develop your relationship with communication you must understand that you have to remain strong. Your perseverance and resistance are what will have those around you navigating towards you. Your communication with yourself, to keep things to yourself and only reveal them when you are ready, is the key to a successful life of communication. How? Easy.

Look when I start out by declaring to the world that I'm starting a business, but don't do anything about it in the following weeks, I am then labeled either as a failure or as having shortcomings. Keep your business to yourself and to those who are involved with whatever it is you are doing. You must—and I repeat—learn to keep silent when you are in a grind-and-hustle mode. I emphasize that so much, because nowadays we want media attention before we even build anything. That isn't communication with the public or your friends, it's being an attention seeker.

Think differently.

The code of silence here really is a separate way of thinking and speaking, where you as a human being working on yourself become one with your inner being. There's a saying in Arabic which roughly translates to "silence is from gold," and sometimes when you are working on yourself, it is best to stay quiet about it. That way when you are complete, and you know you are ready to show the public, everyone is shocked at the final result rather than full of criticism.

When it comes to communication about what it is you want to do to get better, communicate with yourself first and ask yourself if the person you are going to tell your next steps will care or will take the information for their own advantage. You do not want to feel stupid, so keep quiet while you are working and shock the world with the results.

Exit Thoughts

By the time you read a page, an understanding can be formulated; however, if you read it again, you may interpret it differently. The way we are programed to understand issues is so robotic. Between what is said and what isn't, life happens. It hurts to reveal the truth at times, but it should be the way of healing.

I started off this chapter by being motivated by my last relationship. I realized that there was a source of miscommunication that led to a few issues. I then began realizing that communication was far beyond love, a daily process regardless of who we are and what we are doing. I had developed such little understanding of it over the years that had contributed to what I now know. My trauma caused a lot of confusion in my life, and you might be experiencing some of that too. It's okay to go through what you are dealing with, and I hope you know that learning to become a better communicator is an amazing step. I'm proud of you.

I reflected on a lot of aspects of my life recently and found that I might have been the cause of the problem. I didn't like that, hence the reason I wanted to seek help. I am indebted to my therapist and to those around me who understand that at times I am not okay. I wanted to make sure that whoever I was speaking with would understand me. I hope that you as the reader are getting a better image of who I am as a person and the imperfections that really make me who I am.

As we grow older, we start to communicate less and fill up our time with tasks such as work and life. We stop reaching out to people we love because we are busy and slowly but surely get caught up in a rat race. I understand we have problems, and we have our own issues that we are dealing with, but I can't tell you how much it helps if you just reach out to someone to say hello. To ask how they are doing goes a long way.

It has now been 2 months since my recent split, and I can tell you that I barely get any calls or messages from anyone asking me how my day is. I feel lonely at times, but I remember that my parents are still around, so I speak with them. If you have made it this far in the book, please stop right now, pick up your phone, call someone you have not spoken to in a while, and ask how they are. Make things about them for a little bit and watch the satisfaction that you get. Sometimes a small call or a message can light up someone's day in ways that you would have never thought. A random act of kindness will essentially turn your life around. But please, do not do it in expectation that they will return the favor. Do it out the purity of your heart and really be interested.

So many of us are running and forget to stop to count our blessings. Communicate with your loved one before you lose them. Speak your partner's language and learn their body. Communicate through thoughts and express your emotions to your love. It is so important that we realize that we are expressive beings if we choose to be. To your friends and family, communicate, and even if you are at odds now, it is important that you talk it out before it's too late. We are here today and gone tomorrow, and with that, communication can last a lifetime. We live everyday but we only die once. Leave your legacy of peace. When it comes to the hustle, keep your head low and work in silence. Allow yourself to only reveal the master results; that way you can communicate that you are an absolute beast of a worker. You get things done.

All in all, while writing this chapter I have learnt that I still have reasons to learn how to communicate. I am not perfect; I don't think any of us are, but I believe we can learn to become better in hopes of bettering our lives. Learn the unspoken language of your people.

Think. Communicate. Speak.

CHAPTER 9

Salted Wounds

You've been happy before, right? Clapped at weddings, cheered for your teams, laughed with your significant other, and been filled with joy before, no? Would you know happiness if it wasn't for pain? How would pain be defined if we didn't know it's physical embodiment? From breakups to makeups, we are constantly sailing on waves that cause us to feel. It makes us realize that at the end of the day, we are alive. Our senses kick in and we know we should be able to carry on.

Not to toot my own horn, but when it comes to pain, I am an expert. Really, I can tell you stories that would break your heart 10 times over and make you wonder why you thought you considered your issue a problem to begin with. I am speaking from my experience. I bet there's someone out there who can cause me the same feeling. I know you're probably thinking, well, if he thinks my pain means nothing, why am I reading this? That's not what I am saying at all, it's actually the total opposite. I will go through the levels of pain that I have endured over and over again in the last 10 years that have made me thick-skinned, the pain and happiness that has truly made me realize that sometimes it's good to experience it rather than place it to the side.

I know you as the reader have gone through your trials and tribulations as well. You may even be going through it now. Know that I believe your pain is equal to the level of hurt you experienced. I won't be taking away from your hurt but rather letting you in on mine and giving you a different perspective from an immigrant, son, and brother who survived the coldest weather and somehow managed to pull through.

Please do not feel sympathy for me but rather embody my words so that you may understand my hurt. Understand that you are not alone when it comes to pain; none of you are. What we define as pain is only subjective and the opposite of the happiness we once experienced. I have known happiness, an orgasmic, wonderful euphoria of sweet happiness before, and I have seen firsthand the evil the world has to offer. It is only up to us, as battlers on this field of life, to fight to sustain a healthy life.

What is Pain?

You define it. What is it that has caused you to be upset and feel down? Has there ever been a situation that you believe was the outcome of pain but benefited you in the long run?

173

There are different levels or ways that people define pain. It could be that you look at it as heartbreak resulting from a failed relationship, the loss of a family member, failing a test, breaking an arm, someone hurting you, or rather you involuntarily hurting someone. We experience it on so many levels during our day that we sometimes forget to appreciate it. Not succeeding at your job or failing to submit a project on time will give you that feeling of not being good enough, and that in itself is pain. What is pain to you? I have mentioned that word more than 20 times already, and it's because I want to engrave the word in your mind before we continue.

Elevator to Getting Over It

You may think that asking others how to deal with pain will alleviate yours, but it won't. Everyone deals with the opponent of happiness in a different way, and it really is up to you to find out how it is that you can deal with it. I can sit here and give you advice for hours, but it won't resonate with you unless you go through your own trial and error. Now, if you're dealt the consequences of pain, play your hand. Pick a card, a way to deal with it, and play it to see if it helps you deal with your issue. If not, pick another.

Let's look at it in another fashion, one more practical in our lives. Most of us live in buildings or visit friends who live in high-rises, correct? Think of the elevator as a capsule of your pain and the journey you are on that can take you to where you need to be. The first floor may be the level that helps you see your issue in a different manner or rather the level that gives you advice on how to deal with your pain. If the first floor isn't the solution for your problem, take the elevator to the next floor. You may have different elevators for different problems and pains. You may experience trauma which would require a whole different building of solutions. Think of each floor as a solution that you are looking for and experience it as your own. Each floor has a few units, which would be the advice or support you need to get through your issue. Some may be open doors and could welcome you to enter, where you would feel at peace knowing that your pain is understood. Some may close the door in your face as if you're a solicitor trying to introduce a useless product into their life. At the end of the day, it is totally up to you how you want to take that elevator and how you want to knock on the units for emotional support.

One quote my mom always told me to keep in mind is, "People will clap for you when you're happy, but not everyone is willing to stand by you when you are down." I'm 31 years old, and I am finally understanding that exact statement. How it took me the later years of my adult life to get it, I don't know.

I find that I am always categorizing my feelings of pain. I am subject to different kinds of issues on a daily basis, and for the last 10 years it's been a train ride. It really does exhaust you when all you have dealt with in the last couple of years is just a sea of negativity, or rather this opponent I speak of. Sometimes we are placed in this sea of pain without asking for it or expecting it. This is why it's important to remain humble at all times and to realize that you need to consider the fact that your happiness can be gone in seconds.

While on vacation in the Dominican Republic with some friends in June of 2018, I had a conversation with a buddy of mine. We were by the beach, and it was around sunset when we spoke. He had looked at me and said, "Moe, take this in. None of this is going to last forever. We are all happy now, but we really don't know what will hit us in the future and possibly separate us all." I didn't pay that any mind, but low and behold, a year or so later, we all separated and stopped speaking with each other. This was separation pain from a group of friends who were once so tight that we did everything together. This was my building that I had to take the elevator in and realize what I needed to do to get done and get better.

I still think of that conversation to this day every time I see anyone of the members from the old group. I remember the happiness that we once experienced, and it leaves a little space in me knowing it won't ever get back to that. I loved that crew of people; those were great times, but I realized, once I reached a certain floor, that we as humans do not remain stagnant. We are a species that loves to move on and develop further. I found that the older I got, the wiser my floors became. My acceptance of allowing my friends to fly into other relationships that didn't involve me only meant that it was my time to spread my wings and fly as well. I'm sure you have had some friends you are no longer in contact with, not because of any issues or anything, but rather because one of you outgrew the relationship. It's okay, it happens; it's the pain of ending things that causes this emotion.

Let's really dive into the issues at hand and the levels of this opponent that we can feel in our lives. As long as you are breathing, you are subjected to some level of pain. If you can feel happiness, you will recognize it's opposite. Hate it, feel it, love it, but whatever you do don't stop feeling. Welcome to emotional intelligence.

Remember when I mentioned that there are different types of pain that you can feel as a human? Here is how I would define some of them: trauma, heartache, denial, or physical, emotional, and psychological pain. We all deal with these in our own way; however, we may relate in some areas. One thing that I had problems with during the last decade was finding someone to relate to my pain. Some people may understand that you are going through something but not everyone can understand your actual physical and emotional pain. This is okay; not everyone has experienced what you have. In retrospect, this is what makes us so unique, and the irony behind it all is that it makes us beautiful.

Give time, time.

I want you to realize that the evil you may have experienced hasn't solidified into you to becoming that. You may have dealt with the issues then and may have dealt with it now, but you are becoming what you need to be. Know that, know you are beautiful. Do not ever allow anyone to tell you that your pain ain't beauty. There's an underlying reason why you are dealing with what has been given to you. Only time will define this for you. It's also important to note that healing from the situation you are in requires that you give time, time.

In 2010 I was living a normal life, thinking that I had known what pain was. I may have to a certain extent, but I can tell you that I did not know it as I do now. I hadn't experienced much, and I think all of us can relate to the fact that there is just a deeper, stronger pain out there that can destroy us but at the same time build us. That year, I remember hustling, developing myself, and finding out that my job was not one that I wanted to continue. I was working as a truck mechanic, and I was hating it every second of my life, but at the time the money was great. (As I am writing this, I looked at my reflection in the mirror and realized that life has done its number on me. When I looked over at my reflection, I saw that the years that had passed were my youthful years that were taken from me. This is the pain I am currently feeling.)

Back to what I was saying—2010! I recall that I had gone through a small breakup, and I moved on quickly, knowing that it wasn't for me at the time. Everything was normal, and I was living my life as would any 21-year-old. When the new year hit, I remember it being an okay time. It was a snowy night, the night everything in my life changed.

Here's the trauma part that I mentioned earlier that stayed with me till this day and will probably do so for the rest of my life. That night, my little brother Shadi (and for the first time I put this in writing, because I have not said it out loud) passed away. This was pain that I did not think I would experience in a million years. Who thinks that their little or their older brother would suddenly vanish, not existing in physical form? The ability to call my brother and speak to him was no longer an option. I really couldn't speak to him; it was as if I had never had a brother.

I held him in my arms while I called the police for an ambulance with my father. I continuously yelled his name out loud, while slipping my hand down his shirt to feel a heartbeat. He wouldn't answer me. He was still alive; I knew he heard me, but he was slipping away. My little brother that I shared so many memories with and aspirations for the future was now leaving us. I felt so hopeless that I could not help him, that I was not able to be there earlier to prevent it. If there was anyone in our neighborhood that night, they probably heard me screaming from the top of my lungs my brother's name.

When the police showed up, they took him to the hospital and took my mom as well, as she was injured. I was taken to the police station at the time, and while I was in there being interrogated about what happened, I was told that there was some bad news. The bad news was that my little brother had passed away.

Here goes my trauma. From the rest of that night, I remember a few things. The police drove me to the hospital, and when I got out, my friend was walking up to me. I ran towards the entrance, and I dropped to the ground, and he then helped me up. I ran inside not realizing that my whole side was full of blood. I couldn't accept any of it; there was no way that my best friend was gone. What happened? Why did it happen? So many questions unanswered. I hated knowing that he was in pain before he passed. It didn't really click then, until I saw my parents and my mom asked if I was okay. It was that moment that I realized we had become a family of three. (I have to pause here for a moment).

This page has taken me the longest to write. I wasn't able to accept anything that day, and it truly took me some time to accept what was going on that evening. It wasn't easy, and I couldn't fathom the fact that he was gone. This was a new pain for me, one that I had never experienced and one that I never thought I would experience. It was the birth of a new me, a human that is now tarnished for the rest of his life, who knew it would cause me to become who I was. This is the trauma that I carried with me for a very long time.

From then on, I realized, I really knew what pain meant, but I could never place it in a sentence or give it words. I was angry; with trauma comes anger. How was I to deal with this? What was I supposed to do now? Will I ever get over it? The answer to that is simply, "No."

It took me some years to finally come to the realization that I was not going to be okay with accepting it but rather with learning to live with it. I went through so many stages of acceptance, denial, anger, and heartbreak, but none of it pushed me forward. I blamed myself at times, and trust me when I tell you, I was ready to meet my brother in heaven a few times. When I left for Lebanon, I left in distress and wasn't happy that I was leaving the country right away. One week I was living a normal life and the next I was in a foreign country, starting a new life with one less family member.

While in Lebanon, I was forced to deal with my trauma. My mom and I had no one else and no other place to go to. I would see her cry and suffer from the pain that she was in; meanwhile I was silently suffering. I would have family members, strangers in my life, give me advice on how to cope with such issues. The truth is that you cannot give advice on how to deal with certain traumas if you haven't dealt with them yourself. In my mind, the whole world could disappear for all I cared. I just wanted my mom to be okay.

I suffered silently because I did not want my mom worrying about me, and to this day, I am still suffering but in a different way. I would go to sleep listening to my mother cry her eyes out and wake up with her crying. Her baby was taken from her and not in a natural way. She was suffering from the beating she took that night, and to say she wasn't in physical pain would be a lie. That's a strong woman, who dealt with both mental and physical trauma. A year or two into our stay in Lebanon, we began realizing that in order for us to remain on this God forsaken earth, we couldn't give up on life as it would disappoint my brother. I remember after a serious breakdown that my mom and I had, we promised each other that we would hold each other and strengthen the bond to get better. I knew that at that point I could no longer show my weakness to her or my dad. He was dealing with it in his own way, and may God have mercy on his soul, for he suffered so much during that time. I don't know how that man kept it together.

During my last ten years, that was the trauma that I dealt with and can write about. It was one that tested my patience, my mind, my heart, my perseverance, and the ability to keep myself together. At times I feel like I am losing it, and the only thing that pulls me together is the fact that my brother would've slapped me if I did.

There is no way to specifically deal with the trauma of losing a family member. The fact is, it is totally up to you how you deal with it and get over it. The only thing that I can tell you for certain is that it gets easier with time. When I say "easy," I mean that it truly does become a way of your life. You learn to live with the pain that you have experienced and embodied the whole time that you dealt with the issue.

You see, rather than denying it, I said to myself I'm going to accept the fact that it happened to my brother and constantly be in a state of pain. That way I don't deny it, and everything I do from now on will be in honor of him and the success he would have wanted. What people didn't know or don't know till this day is that I daydream. I can be out on a rooftop patio, drinking and having a great time, and meanwhile I am imagining my brother being there with me enjoying it all. I have never for a second in the past ten years lived a day without the thought of my brother by my side. His absence has allowed me to realize that pain runs so deep in my blood that happiness becomes the most appreciated thing. When you lose all that you have, you learn to forgive easily. The beautiful thing about pain is that once you experience it, you learn to appreciate all that's around you.

From that pain, I began having attachment issues. I started to really develop the mentality that it is easy for me to walk away from something that no longer serves me, as I have already experienced the biggest loss in my life. I knew that it didn't matter who walked into my life or walked out of it; I was alone anyway. This wasn't a healthy type of pain, and I urge you, if you find yourself in a place of solitary emotional confinement, to do something to leave it. This mentality that I had only allowed those who would have benefited my life to walk right out of it. I was very careful with who I let into my life and what they knew about me. A lot of my friends wouldn't understand why I was the way I was but that wasn't up to them. It was my life, and let's face it, I wasn't okay. What I did next helped me, though. I began giving people a chance. I was never ready for love or new relationships with people. I would be in disguise, and everything that I had on me was registered to an alias. The name MRFRANKG on my Instagram was the alias that I had developed when I was back in Toronto. People really knew me as Frank, and the idea of Moe was gone.

Dealing with my trauma in stages, I shelled myself out for the first couple of years, as I did not want to deal with anyone or anything. This took quite a long time but, hey, I wasn't ready. When you're dealing with your trauma, know that it is okay to take all the time in the world. Nothing is escaping you, and if your faith in God or whatever you believe in is strong, you too will get through this. Once I realized that pushing people out only made me lonelier, I started allowing people back into my life. I started dating again, but I had my reservations. I wasn't talking about my brother or opening up about him, and to this day, with anyone I date, I would not mention it unless it was serious.

I urge of you, though, if you are going through any sort of pain, allow yourself to go through it. Do not stop and place it to the side. Sidelining the pain or issue you are dealing with will only delay your process of healing. When you are ready to share with the world, the world is ready to hear you. Do not let anyone tell you otherwise. It is also important to allow your heart to love again. Nothing heals a wounded heart but love.

I slowly declined my presence in the area of attachment issues. I began realizing that life is so precious, and it can be taken from me at any moment. This is when I started acting and thinking differently. I started reflecting back to when my brother was alive and what I could have done differently. If I could go back, I would be ten times more giving and loving towards him. I would give all that I could to know he was happy with me and his family, even more than he already was.

This emotion came when it was too late, however, and that's what hurts the most. As human beings we really don't appreciate the life around us until it is gone. That's why you hear people say, "I'm sorry I wasn't there for such and such. If I could only hear your voice ..." Look, do all that you would wish to do while they're still alive, because the pain of regret is so much more than the pain of failure. If you have an ounce of love in your heart, please give that out to someone today rather than when it's too late.

I'm a firm believer, and I say this with passion, that people skip the fact that they need to be there for someone while we're still alive. If I pass, I wouldn't want anyone who wasn't there for me before showing me love and support after I leave.

Where was all this when I was alive? That's why it's important to support the people around while they're still here. I slowly began adopting this mentality, and it's hard for people to understand, but I began to do things as if tomorrow isn't promised.

My pain because of the evil brought me something beautiful. Although not understood by many, I kept on being myself. Whether it was a love relationship or a friendship, I promised myself that I would not go to sleep or have any of my friends go to sleep with tension between us. It wasn't for myself; it was the promise I had made with life. The pain that I had experienced I didn't want to experience again. If you ask my previous love, she'll tell you that if there was ever an argument, I always wanted to solve it before we went to sleep. I was never okay with the fact that the next day one of us may not be there. I did not want to leave any wounds open to be salted.

I started loving more and developing an appreciation for people. If there was a time where I knew care was needed, I jumped to it. I began to become vulnerable so that I would allow people to feel the love. I guess in a way I wanted to make the world a better place by offering all that I could've offered Shadi. It may have been overwhelming for some, but I knew that if I was to move on in this life, I would be remembered for the feeling of care that I provided. If you were in my life previously and wondered why I am the way I am, you have just received your answer.

Is pain really the answer to happiness?

How can yin be appreciated without yang? The balance we need is found in pain. Without the feeling associated with it, the ability to know happiness would not exist. Would we know the appreciation of love if not for heartbreak? Or the smile that wrinkles our face that once had tears on our cheeks? Have you dealt with heartbreak before? Would you know what that was without the ultimate price of love?

Look, I spoke about my trauma and what I did to get out of it. I was being 100% raw with you about it all. Somehow my previous pain turned into the love that I gave people. With the love that I initiated came the fact that sometimes love can break as well. This heartbreak allowed me to realize how I need to act in this instance of pain.

I had a conversation with a family friend of mine last night, and I knew I had to continue writing this chapter today. I hadn't seen her in forever, and we decided to catch up for old times' sake. It's funny how sometimes you can go months and years without seeing someone, but when you finally do, it's like you never left. She started talking to me about everything, and we slowly got into the conversation of how life has played out for me. She said no matter what you and your parents do, trouble always seems to find you guys. There's not one year that has passed by in the last decade that you all weren't in some kind of pain. How you are actually surviving now is beyond me. What she didn't understand is that when you have no choice, your pain becomes your melodic driving force. The songs to the days you live are sung through the pain you have experienced.

Now you may not get this but pay attention to the next time you step outside and how you go about your actions throughout the day. I told her that my life in the last 10 years wasn't easy, and by no means am I taking away from my pain. I don't say things like, "Some people have it worse," because that takes away from my actual suffering, and that's not right. People who say, "It could be worse," or "Some people have it worse," need to shut up. I repeat that. If you say those two sentences to someone who is explaining their suffering or their severity of pain, you need to re-evaluate your mentality. It takes away from their emotional pain and does not rectify your misunderstanding about the trauma they are dealing with.

In my conversation with my friend, I began to open up about my recent breakup, the breakup that had me realizing I had achieved unconditional love. Let's not equate unconditional love with happiness, because it brings a level of pain with it too. The feeling of loving somebody so much, regardless of what they did to you or where they are in the world, is one that is fulfilling but at the same time so painful.

She looked at me and said, "But you've been through so much. A failed engagement that had you so upset that you didn't recover for at least a few months back in 2015." I started thinking about that pain and the category of "Love:Pain" started really resonating. We all have failed relationships, some that taught us well and some that were absolute shams. Although that relationship was not one that I am proud of, it taught me one thing: I did not have unconditional love for that person as I had not achieved that level of pain yet. When you truly get hit with pain from love, you either hate the person or you love the person so much that you feel a tiny bit of pain from that excess love.

After that split in 2015, I wanted nothing but to move on. That was my main goal. I was a free bird again, unchained from such an exhausting set of events. This pain was temporary, and now that I look back at it, there were signs I gave to myself that showed me it was temporary. We sometimes don't understand the lessons pain gives us right away. It may take some time, it may take a lifetime for that matter, but patience is key.

My friend went through a divorce at around the same time, and I witnessed his pain, which was on a totally different scale. While he was in the midst of leaving his wife, he kept telling me that as long as she was happy, he'd be happy. I thought he was crazy. He was no longer with her, so why did he care about her happiness? I kept telling him to move on, and even though he eventually did, till this day he says that all he wants for her is to be happy and okay. He explained to me that this is his undying, unconditional love for her as a human being. Circa 2015, I was oblivious to what this all meant, but here we are, and here's why I gave you the background as I introduced the main character.

You live and learn.

I know pain firsthand. Physical and mental, emotional, and soulful pain that has affected me throughout the years. I introduced a little bit of a background before to introduce you to the art of painting pain from love. Through my last break up, I had mentioned in the previous chapters that I had split with my forever love. At this moment, that is the situation for me. After my breakup I realized a few things. My pain was not temporary but permanent. Regardless of your ethnicity, race, culture, or sexuality, you all have experienced breakup pain, so I know you can relate.

What ended up happening is that I went through my phases of emotions, anger, hate, resentment, not to mention a few that I am keeping out of the loop. These were fueled by my thoughts of what happened and what was causing this whole fiasco. After a while I somehow returned to who I am, and I guess it comes full circle once you experience it all and allow the pain to run through your body. You become yourself again. I realized that I was mad at myself and was running away from the truth this whole time. I did want to love unconditionally and didn't want to continuously feel a one-sided love for a relationship that was no more. I was running away from the truth (and sometimes we all are).

Sometimes we don't have it in us to accept the reality of a situation and so we continuously keep running away from it. We don't want to admit it, and we don't want to face it. This is one of the side effects of pain. I knew and now realize that this effect of my past isn't a healthy one. You also may be dealing with pain differently now because of what has happened to you but know that it doesn't define you. Pain caused previously can never become your definition of life.

I don't know you, but I know that as a human being you are capable of overcoming your situation. I had my brother pass away in my arms, I have had family members and friends speak ill of my family while we were at our lowest, I have been thrown into a third-world country with no plan, I came back to Canada not having a plan and being a ghost, and I started losing those closest to me because of my past. So, I understand my pain has a lot to do with how I handle things now, but I know it does not define me.

For what is love if not an embrace and lips that sing beautiful melodies when touched?

What I was running from was the advancement of my feelings and my leveling up as a human being. I was now achieving a new level of love from all the pain I have experienced, and it was dedicated to the human I was no longer with. This is one of the benefits of pain and the side effects: pain can make you feel again. I realized that no matter what they did or how they did it, or rather where they were or who they were with, as long as they were happy, I was happy.

I am not a slave for love, and I don't think any of us are, but I am a human being who is in love with someone for more than just their looks, personality, or demeanor. The night I really realized I had unconditional love, I had drunk half a bottle of Virginia Black and really got into my feelings. I promised myself that I was not going to run away from my pain anymore. I cried that night. I was crying because I had run away from my acknowledgement of this love and hid it in excuses. I cried because I was running away from so much of my past pain that now had built up and been brought to light. I had not known how to accept my brother not being there for me, and it was so hard to say that I had unconditional love for anyone else, but I did for her.

I could then say with total confidence that as long as she was happy with whatever she was doing in her life, I was a happy man. I knew that my pain from my past had taught me to appreciate a good soul, an innocent being, and an aura only God can give. It was fine for me; I came to terms with it and started transitioning into "being at peace." Loving unconditionally may bring pain, don't get me wrong, but you must know that your love must be greater than the pain.

Some may have the misconception that a good guy can be taken advantage of. Can they really be taken advantage of if the person that is doing good is doing it out of the kindness of their heart? You really cannot phase someone who is doing something without expectations. Sometimes love can be the greatest cure to all diseases and somehow it can be the worst cancer. Projections of a relationship really do depend on the bond of love we can provide each other. These outcomes are based on the type of effort and income that we place into it from the get-go.

Understanding that love isn't easy, it is best to know that pain is associated with loving someone. We grow up our entire lives accustomed to our family, and somehow within months of meeting someone, we realize we want to spend the rest of our lives with them. We must understand that in order to endure such longevity we need to precondition our brain with the pros and cons of falling in love. Seeing a future with someone will never be rainbows and sunshine. The ups and downs will befall you, but it is up to you as to how you want to love the pain.

Some may say that this pain is unnecessary, but is it? Do we know love without hate? Or push without shove? Hard without soft? Wounds heal, they never stay open, and with time everything gets better. What we need to do is not pour any salt on these wounds.

At times we run away from pain, not realizing that the side effects that come along with it can be the life lesson we have been waiting to learn. You must understand that not everything is revealed right away. Some situations take time to mix and marinate in your life, and you must wait. If your heart break is existing now, wait. Do not push away from the pain or away from what it has caused you to feel. It is important that you do this so that when the lesson appears and pops up in front of you, you are prepared for it.

We feel as humans, on a daily basis, no matter where we go or what we do. Allow your emotions to run through your veins, to be pumped throughout your body and to continuously move you. These side effects are some that you may have already experienced and some that you would have never thought would be true. Remember when you were a kid? Remember when you fell down and experienced pain? What happened after that? You learned what not to do so that you don't experience this pain again. I wonder sometimes why it is that we adults repeat the same mistakes expecting different outcomes, knowing the pain we have already experienced.

As kids, we knew not to do something twice because it hurt, whether it was saying something rude to someone or a physical act that actually caused us pain. We were disciplined to the point where the pain was so temporary that none of us really remember much of it. I believe that as adults we tend to mitigate the risk as we grow older. I for one have found that I have repeated the same mistakes over and over again when I've already experienced the pain. I am not sure why, but I find that I give people and situations second chances. I see the good in people that they may not already see. Sometimes pain brings out the beauty in you, so it's important that you do not shy away from such agony.

Beauty to the Beast

You are in no way horrible because of your pain or what you have experienced in your life. War wounds that we acquire are representations of the trials and tribulations that we had to deal with to become the strong men and women we are today. Who are we to even judge what someone has gone through? We at times belittle someone's pain because we either don't understand it or don't give it time to get into our heads.

That is why it is key that we understand that people are affected by pain that we may not understand. We must always account for that rather than what our agenda dictates to us. You yourself may have hidden pain that you are quiet about. Would you want someone to totally disregard it, as though it meant nothing, and to belittle it? When we speak, we must think not only about our response but also include empathy about how the individual may receive it.

I can't tell you how many times someone has launched a full attack at me, because of their own frustration, without realizing that I have been dealing with so much pain. Most of us don't understand things unless we see it or hear it. We simply don't consider it. It's time for that change.

I remember a part of my 2020 and 2021, when I was dealing with so much pain. It was due to so many factors. Someone reached out to me in such a rude way, but then realized that what they did was wrong and justified it by saying they were dealing with a lot, not knowing that I was having suicidal thoughts and was just not happy in general. I never admitted how I was feeling, however I did set boundaries.

When people don't gauge what you may be dealing with and simply approach you in a harmful manner, you need to set your boundaries too. Even though they can be going through it as well, that does not give them the right to project their insecurities or pain onto you, and neither should you treat anyone else that way.

Now, when I say these thoughts were coming to me, I mean that I was just fed up with life. During my brother's 10-year anniversary, I had gone to my parents for a bit. Walking up to the front door, everything flashed in front of me. it was like it was January 24, 2011, all over again. I stood there and looked in between the houses, only to remember what happened. (When I walk up to the house, till this day, I remember how cold it was and the screaming I did to get my brother conscious again.) This is pain that is systemic and will forever stay with me.

The way that I have learnt to deal with this pain and attempt to heal from it is to continuously feel it. I don't want to forget this pain as it has taught me so many lessons. I am healing till this day and will continue to do so. I am taking my pain day by day and learning along the way. I believe I can be a great man by achieving the small tasks and learning to fix my mistakes. I believe you can do this too. Learn to live with your pain day-by-day and minute-by-minute. Face your pain and realize that it is okay to go through it rather than hiding it. Confrontation in this case can be your best buddy when dealing with bringing pain and unhealed emotion to the surface.

Exit Thoughts

Even though I find that the world has been nothing but evil in the last couple of years, I find that it is within me as a human to still look at life as beautiful. When Shadi passed away, a large part of me went missing. My innocence as a young adult was taken. I realized I can either hate the world or do what my brother was doing, showing love. My relationships after that year were always up and down with no consistency. I realized shortly after that it was my pain speaking to me, asking me to heal. It wasn't really until 2021 that I started seeking help that I saw some improvement.

Every day I see people lunge at others with total disregard of what someone else is going through. Sometimes it's important to realize that it isn't up to society to depict or dictate how pain affects you or how you deal with it. You must allow time to take its course and for the lessons to come to light. Don't rush into learning what the lesson was or why it was given to you. It wasn't until years later that I learned how to maneuver the pain that was given to me from 2011. It truly was a shower of evil that was sent to me and started my journey to a life that I now place in this book. It's as If I was standing in a storm of evil rain with my umbrella, awaiting my destiny.

Be empathetic towards people. You never know who is healing, who is dealing with pain, and who is attempting to become great again. We all have our breaking points. To assess others' thresholds as anything less than the levels they have encountered would not be right.

If you are healing now from an incident of some sort, know it takes time. Know that you must find your own way of getting through. If you have found this chapter to be of some help, then my job here is 50% complete. The other 50% is for you to accomplish with hard work. You will find yourself in the ups and downs of emotion, but I believe that you can do it. At the end of the day, 10 years later, I am still alive and still managing to get by day-by-day. I leave you this: you are not defined by your trauma but by the future that awaits you.

CHAPTER 10

Keeping the Peace

With everything happening around us, it's really tough nowadays to continuously be at peace. Every situation that you face has the opportunity to alter your bubble of solitude. To be honest I think we all realize now more than ever that the factors that attack us keep us working overtime for everything that doesn't aid us. This can range from talk, actions, and messages to trauma, surroundings, and situations. We never know what tomorrow holds, and that in itself can keep us worrying and affect our peace. The goal is to remain at ease, with a sense of security that allows us to live our normal lives.

In this chapter, I'll be touching on the pillars of this idea. Part of what I have been using to stay sane with every situation I have dealt with is **adjusting, reshaping, blocking/walking, and developing** for peace. I wrote about the 5 pillars of control; this is my theory of the hand of peace. We all have the world in the palms of our hands, and we can use this peace for our own benefit.

It's ironic that as I am writing this chapter, my mind and soul are not at peace. You may wonder how is it that I am attempting to write to you, to get a point across, while I myself am not at ease right now. I wrote about pain in my previous chapter, about how we use it to appreciate happiness, while I was suffering and in pain. Here we need to apply the same concept, being at war with your inner being in order to appreciate your peace later. Whoever said being at peace was an easy process lied to you, me, and all of us.

Tame the beast within.

Being at peace with others let alone yourself is a serious struggle. We are influenced day in and day out by the outside forces of this world that tend to place our peace at war. The trick is to win small battles along the way and eventually win the war during your life. You will be subjected to opinions, words, and (more dangerously) actions of others when your peace is being attacked. What is found within us though is the ability to muster the courage to block all this out without realizing where the energy came from. This energy comes from your past battles, which you fought in order to maintain your healthy mentality, with the battle scars that have been imbedded in your personality, your soul, and more importantly your inner peace beast.

197

You may have read in the previous chapters the relatable "beast" idea. Whether it was regarding communication, risk, control, or positivity, the beast in you can cater to all aspects. There is one exception, however. If the beast is not at peace, none of the previous concepts I have explained will come easily. Your positivity will be affected in ways that will absolutely overwhelm you. Your control will be swayed, loosening the grip you may have on whatever it is that is destroying you. The risk you take is no longer calculated but rather mitigated in a sloppy fashion. The communication that you may be experiencing will be one of anger and frustration.

All of the previous beasts that I have spoken about will be at arm's length, waiting to lunge into action if your inner beast (being) is not at peace. This is why it is so key that we keep our mind in check and develop a sense of how we are to relieve the stress that we are dealing with. I myself am at war with a very specific aspect at this current moment in time. For some reason I cannot find the middle ground where my heart and mind can meet.

For many years now I have been continuously introduced to aspects of destructive peace, aspects that idolize havoc and chaos, which I would never choose. Their traits can be shape shifting and arrive at different times of the day or in different ways, from people speaking or talking to me in certain ways about certain issues, to situations that cause my very essence to be disturbed.

I think we can all agree that, in 2021, we are reformulating ourselves, revaluating ourselves and redeveloping the very structure that has made us. What we have been through, as the human race, are 2 of the worst years that we have witnessed. Every aspect of our lives has been attacked and affected by this pandemic. Healthy relationships are no more, mentally strong individuals have slowly felt the wrath, communication has declined, and therapists are making a lot of money. This pandemic has destroyed the peace the world once lived in and adapted to over the years.

So where do we go from here? Have you all been feeling your unsettled peace? I know I have. So many things can and have contributed to this uneasy feeling, but it is up to us to regain control of it. We can, believe it or not, be at peace again with the world and with ourselves. I will be touching on what we can do to attain that feeling once again; however, in the meantime, I'll take you through my journey of destruction and my war-winning mentality.

Foundation = Peace

Growing up we never had a solid place we called home because we moved around every couple of years. This not only created an anxious state of mind, it also didn't provide us the peace required as kids. We always knew that we couldn't build anything solid for a few years because we would have to move again. Mind you, our parents were trying to make things work, and with limited resources, they did the best that they could. I'm sure their world was at war also, not to mention the events that caused their lives to constantly be at war later.

The effects of this never really made their way to surface until years later, and we noticed it when we got a little older. We always attempted to search for that one missing piece that would create our long-desired peace. A few years after this we had experienced the ultimate peace-breaker. I'm sure if you recall your history, you will find the one instance that broke your peace and flipped your life upside down. I'm also sure that, if you analyze your parents' lives, you'll realize that they dealt with destruction and a life with no peace at one point. Their sacrifices to come to the place where they lived and to make a name for themselves were very hard. It's tough to even think about how they dealt with so many life-altering decisions that always kept them on edge. The new generation isn't willing to give up half of what they did in order to advance and make it in life.

The rise is difficult; the decline is easy.

You must realize that you will be spending some time reorganizing, as destruction is easier than reconstruction. Once it all comes crumbling down, take a step back and breathe. The one thing that I found to help in dire times is not attempting to make any immediate decisions when engulfed in anger. The reason behind this thinking is that anger is the direct result of a chaotic presence. We tend to always want to act on our emotions or allow them to dictate our future. This is where your ego and pride need to be in check. The moment someone cannot get to those two sides of yourself, your peace is undeniably untouched. You're golden.

What happens in an argument is that there are usually two opinions that are going back and forth about a topic. The first person to lose their cool usually loses completely. But remain cool, allow your thoughts to get organized, and check in. If you're wondering, "How Is it that I can do this?" go back and read about control again. You must master your self-control, whether in your mind, heart, or soul. Do not go into combat with someone who is at peace with themselves. You may win that battle, but the war is in their favor.

What we sometimes fail to understand (and it's the reason I left this topic to the end) is that being at one with yourself is the main aspect that will allow you to live. Finding your reason in life will become so much easier the moment you realize that all you have manifested has now become your reality. I spent the majority of 2015 to 2016 working on myself after my breakup. What I said to myself was that I needed to adopt a new lifestyle, a new career, perhaps, and become a little more in tune with who I am. The biggest mistake was that I allowed myself to lose my peace.

While I was on my discovery trip, I learned that I was almost at peace with myself. The only thing that was keeping me up at night was losing my brother. I can tell you that even with that I had started reformatting my brain to understand the situation a little differently. I was beginning to understand that I couldn't blame myself for it anymore. There was no way that I could have prevented it, and even though I ran the same scenario in my head over and over again for 4 or 5 years, nothing changed. My brother was gone, and I was still living with the pain of his leaving. So, I said to myself, "I need to adjust my thinking and truly start blocking out these negative thoughts that are coming in from all angles."

Tune in: adjust.

Now that I am writing this chapter, I am realizing I was performing the pillars of attaining peace that I mentioned in the beginning: adjusting, reshaping, blocking/walking, and developing. I adjusted my attitude by reshaping my physical being while blocking out any negative thoughts, which allowed me to develop. The hardest part about all this is walking the talk. I can only talk so positively or try to change my mentality about situations so much, but without actually doing the work, my world of peace was always at war.

Developing the mentality of realizing that you need to adjust for your own peace is not simple. Your understanding of what is causing your disturbance needs to be transparent enough that you can point it out. This only at times happens when you dive in too deep, or it consumes you.

Leaving the country just 14 days after my brother departed was my cue to adjust. Getting to Lebanon and beginning a new life disturbed my inner being. It was probably the most confused I had ever been. I was fighting my inner demons, negative thoughts, the built-up curiosity about what happened, and questions that weren't answered. What was I to do? Sometimes we find ourselves in a whirlwind of confusion of emotions and thoughts. Is this really the time to adjust the thought process?

When you find yourself forcefully placed in an environment that does not serve you in a positive manner, adjust. Start with the smallest of tasks that will help you with the larger picture. These small maneuvers will allow for a compound effect to develop within your life.

Adjust your physical being by removing yourself from what is causing this chaos.

Adjust your thought process by thinking in a different manner.

Adjust your speech and how you respond to the situation. Sometimes silence is golden.

Adjust your reaction. Not every situation requires your reaction. The moment you react to it you give it attention.

Adjust your hearing. Develop a knack for what you want to interpret from a conversation.

Adjust your manner and how you deal with the situation.

Adjust your soul. Alleviate the pain by thinking of a happy place.

The above steps aren't in order, but they are a way to create your peaceful space again. Once your space is invaded, it is important that you start adjusting to the parasites that have entered into your life. What we want needs work and effort. Realize that no one is willing to help you on your journey but yourself.

This is why it is key that you exert your effort by yourself to change in your peaceful surrounding. This surrounding can be your mind, body, soul or even physical space. Do not get comfortable with endangering your bubble of peace. The moment you allow any of these externalities to enter into your life, or you let go of any red flags you see, you are slowly allowing your foundation to crumble. The red flags we disregard in the beginning of any situation become the red flags that either destroy us or have us walk away completely.

I really don't think that we should wait for a catastrophe to become a better version of ourselves or rather to be at peace. This is a never-ending process and should be a major focus throughout our lives. We must realize that while we are experiencing the rough terrain that we are traveling on, we must always work on keeping the peace within us. It isn't easy, but it isn't hard either.

Finding the balance between your ideas to execute a peaceful transition or mindset can only come from witnessing what you do not want. Taking control of that is powerful, and it may define who we are as human beings. When you allow red flags to wave freely in disregard, you will allow the disrespect to enter your life. This isn't physical, but you start eroding the quality of love you give or are willing to receive.

When the object of your time or love is not willing to understand that the idea of peace comes from a place of love, they, too, will cause chaos, and this is when you must adjust. You must adjust your speech, your actions, your demeanor, and most importantly your outlook on the situation. Do not let anger or frustration cloud your judgement. This will only bring resentment, and you will be destroying your own peace. Instead allow your peace to create love for the other party. Allow love to consume you, bringing you self-love, bringing you self-peace.

The danger is not within chaos but within the power of inner peace. You must understand that the strongest of men and women will be those who confidently take actions that come from inner peace. This might never have been the case within their lives, but they have allowed themselves to develop the ability to decline anything that affects their inner peace. I know through my situations that when it comes to making key, life-altering decisions, it is best that we make them from a place of dangerous peace. Being at one is never a weak trait. The moment you know yourself is the moment you become unstoppable.

Take a pottery class: reshape.

Through adjusting comes the work of reshaping your being. The fact that you have adjusted to new territories or allowed these outside enabling factors to stop entering into your life means you are now in the reshaping stage. This stage is critical, and it does take time, so do not be disheartened, you'll get through it. As always, I will be including some of my own personal experiences so that you recognize the similarities that you may have in your life.

Who doesn't want inner peace, to be at peace with where they are in life, who they are with, what they are doing, while sleeping better at night and developing a life worth leaving behind? We all do. We want it so much that we are willing to become selfish; however, that isn't the right way to go about it.

Reshaping your life really starts at your core. You must realize that sometimes we shift from the values and morals that we have been taught and have built on. This is okay. You and I are not perfect, but what imperfections we have can create the space to grow into greatness. Now when we form this distance it is key that we reflect. When you find yourself acting out of your range of values, take a step back, reflect immediately, assess, and act. This will help you quickly reshape yourself into the being that you once knew, who held these highly-respected standards.

I have been in this boat before, multiple times. Believe me when I tell you it takes great strength to form discipline toward whatever it is that is in front of you and not betray your core beliefs. If you find yourself at the edge of this betrayal, stop and ask yourself if this is who you are and what you stand for. I bet it isn't, so reshape. Reshape the situation to reflect you and only you.

Although our past does not define us, it does teach us. It allows us to come to terms with what we want and most importantly what we don't want. This is life's way of shaping you into the human being you are today. Believe me when I tell you that destiny has a weird way of shaping your future. I was exposed to this exact situation where I found myself continuously asking if this was really what I stood for. Why did I preach and not follow through?

When you begin reshaping your life do not let guilt be the reason you start. Allow the right logic to become the force behind this change. You must realize that reshaping your inner peace can come in three forms. Either you are reshaping your inner peace from your past, your present, or your future. They all intertwine, so don't think that any of those three won't have an effect on you. Your past inner peace will affect your present, and if your present is affected, your future is in jeopardy as well. Notice that I have tied all these items within one thing: yourself. Allow your past to come to reality. Remember: you are not who yesterday declared you to be. And today you are being reborn.

The only way that we can reshape our past to bring inner peace to our present self is to accept the situations we have been in. This isn't easy, as pain lasts a lifetime, and I truly understand that. I, till this day, daydream about my brother. When I am driving, I clear up any clutter on the passenger seat as I envision him sitting beside me. When I'm at home, I envision him knocking on my door and coming over like he owned the place. When I need help with something, I daydream about calling him, as he is still in my favorites list in my phone.

I realize that my pain now has been reshaped. The way my brother passed was not a natural one and in no way was it not traumatic. I have allowed myself to live with the pain and will continuously live with it; however, I had to reshape my mentality about accepting that it happened, and that I couldn't have done anything to prevent it. At times, though, I weaken the walls of my fortress of inner peace by allowing the negative thoughts to enter again. Am I failing? No. I am simply not allowing my values and core morals to shine through.

What I learned from this process is that I have to remember my roots and the lessons my father taught my brother and me. I, till this day, reshape my inner peace by remembering the reason I am alive. I reshape it by realizing I am alive for my brother, to continue his legacy and to support my family. That is a weight that I must not take lightly or fail to carry. What I am doing here is finding a reason to help me reshape my thought process and to continue the inner peace that my past tried to endanger. I am not my past but rather the lessons that my past has taught me.

You have it in you to reshape the human being that you are and to be peaceful. Allow your soul to heal. Allow your actual being to reshape itself and attune to a calm place. I know you may think that your past dictates your present or future, but I promise you it doesn't. Your trauma does not need to be as unhinged as mine. You can have your own experiences, and you may have had even more traumatic events. The toxicity will only travel into your presence if you allow it to move in.

This is where your mental strength comes in. Even though we may find ourselves at the trough of a wave of mental weakness, reshaping your mind is just one step away. Recognize what leads to your past becoming chaotic and what began the destruction. If you can start pointing out these events and their catalysts, you are already one step ahead. Don't start thinking about what the old you did and how ashamed you are of it. The fact is that everyone has a different version of us in their minds. Point out the enablers of your past, the ones that brought nothing but bad vibes that altered yours. Find out what didn't work and begin using it as a tool for your reshaping.

When you enter a pottery class you are given a few items to use to make the item of your choice. Sitting at a potter's wheel, you are given clay, water, an apron, and some possible instructions. Think of your life and the reshaping of your inner peace as making a clay object at this pottery class. The apron is a symbol of protection from all foreign elements you are using to reshape your inner being. The clay in itself will not form into any object without your hands and water. These elements, when used with the instructions, will allow you to form whatever it is you set your mind to.

Hopefully reading this book will give you the value you are looking for. Begin by regaining the consciousness of peace you are aching to develop again. Start by identifying what you want to protect. Is it your values and what you stand for? Great, then wear that like an apron to help protect you from everything that is coming your way. Now you must choose the next elements that will help you develop this object of peace. Are they new friends, new surroundings, new ways of thinking, or new eating habits? Choose 2 or 3 things at a time that you believe will be tangible for your future.

Now live in the present and begin molding these elements into your object or subject of peace. Begin by taking the first steps in reshaping your life and noticing what you need to add. While shaping the clay, you sometimes have to add more pressure to get a cleaner wall or more water so that you can extend the clay. Is your life not in the same process of reshaping, where you constantly have to add more elements to provide yourself with inner peace? Do you not place pressure on yourself to develop stronger walls that will not crumble when that toxicity commences in your life or when the negative thoughts start developing? Once you have started thinking of what is required for you to live a toxin-free life you become resistant to what doesn't serve you.

You will notice that your "apron" gets dirty from time to time as the process of creation itself is messy. Be conscious of your surroundings and who is paying attention to your bubble of happiness. Those around you may not want that for you, as they have not attained it themselves. When you notice this, your approach to thinking about how to react needs to come from a place of peace. You are developing a great aspect of your life that others may want, and you can help. Reshaping your physical being only comes with the hands that reshaped your mentality. Once you finish molding your object of peace, place it in a furnace and let it cure. This is the key aspect of patience. Realize that inner peace takes time and that reshaping who you are into a castle of solid fortitude takes time. It takes curing, and life itself will allow you to bond all the elements together to cultivate a long-lasting, peaceful existence.

Stop and Go: Blocking/Walking

Adjusting and reshaping may not be for everyone, but they are essential steps to restarting your journey on the road to regaining peace. The art of blocking is not easy to achieve. Sometimes our surroundings do not allow us to block the energy we don't require, and sometimes we place ourselves in non-energetic pods. These pods do not define us, but they do help break us down further, thereby destroying our inner peace.

It is also important to know what it is you need to block out of your life. Assess the life you live and what isn't adding to your health. Is it your friends? Your social life? Your way of living? Your health? Your diet? This is like a 4-way stop: you come to the stop, and you assess who goes first. If you allow the wrong individual to go ahead first, you may end up in an accident that isn't beneficial for anyone. This is the process that you need to learn to develop: blocking and walking.

Walking doesn't mean walking away from the situation or individual that is causing this distortion but rather carrying out the actions that you intended. Know that if you are on a path of inner peace, you must set some goals for yourself. These goals are only going to be plausible if you act on them, hence the idea of walking. When you are walking towards your goal of peace, know that it will take some time for you to decide the design of your actionable goals. Blocking all outer actions and thoughts that come your way is your next step to achieving what is required to become the next, best version of yourself.

Now there may be times when you need to walk away from situations or people, and that is okay. Walk away with your dignity, with respect and honor. Do not walk away leaving a negative void in someone's life. Do not leave a negative impression as it will harm you in the long run. Most of us decide to walk away without realizing the damage we are causing to the opposing party.

I suffer from anxiety, bad anxiety, and from panic attacks. No one has really seen me suffer from panic attacks, but my anxiety is something that I cannot hide at times. These issues stem from my trauma and my past experience through thoughts that come to mind. I have realized over the years that it is me who holds these thoughts captive. If I allow the gates of my mind to remain open, these destructive thoughts come marching in. I start thinking of the what ifs, the maybes, and the future outcome of situations that don't and won't ever exist.

You see, it wasn't just 2011 that became the catalyst to my what ifs, but also an earlier incident that nearly changed my life again. My mother, God bless her soul, was another reason that I had thought my life was going to change. In 2017 she had gone in for surgery, and during recovery she had flat-lined for a few seconds. I was standing by her side and the nurse came in to change her I.V. (I believe), and I stepped out. A few minutes later, while I was outside, I heard the nurses yelling to my mom, and the whole hospital went into Code Blue. Standing outside, I started to calmly freak out. Doctors and nurses running into my mom's room and yelling out her name while I waited outside patiently observing all that happened.

I was crouched down, back against the wall, and for some reason I began silently to panic. I remembered 2011, the yelling I did for my brother, and how he didn't wake back up. My father wasn't at the hospital at that time, so it was just me.

211

The family of the neighboring patient was asked to stay outside, and what I did not know was that they were asking me if I was okay and talking to me; but it was as if a bomb had gone off, and my ears were just ringing.

Twenty minutes later I was allowed in, and I saw my mother. The moment I realized she was breathing and conscious, I felt like my world was normal again. I realized at that moment that I could've easily been without a mother, and I wasn't sure If I would be able to handle losing another loved one.

Things began changing once again after that, and my thoughts began walking through the open gates of my mind. My anxiety almost immediately went all the way back up. I wasn't blocking the negative thoughts anymore; my mind was weak. I was allowing anything and everything to enter, hence my mentality of peace was now destroyed. My mind became incarcerated once again in the jail of my surroundings. What was I to do? I hate losing loved ones. Once you feel you might lose someone, you begin to value the life you're living now. I wanted out; I wanted my mind to be free again. What was I supposed to do?

If there is one thing I've learned in the last 2 years, it's that the negative thoughts you have are not to be shared. I was allowing the what ifs of tomorrow to take refuge within my life. The life I needed to live now was not one I was living. I was consumed by fear and doubt instead of being full of confidence and certainty. This was me walking away from what I needed to do to become great again.

Red Light, Green Light

Now that I have given you a small glimpse of my personal life, let me explain what helped me. The walking and blocking that helped move forward and attain the peace that I so longed for began when I looked the other way. When we allow just about anything into our lives, we become unorganized, from the food that we eat, what we drink and the TV that we watch. Nothing developed for the advancement of the human mind involved stagnancy. This is why mental health is a serious topic during the pandemic. We ate and developed COVID weight, watched Netflix endlessly and did not exercise. We were not able to develop ourselves into positive, productive human beings. We opened up the gates, but our brains were incarcerated. Admitting to yourself that you have fallen off the bandwagon is the first step. Knowing what you need to do to get better is the next step.

You must literally block out all energy that does not serve you. If you must stop someone from saying something negative, do it. Sometimes it's best to not even reply to that ounce of toxicity coming your way. You have to start walking away from these temporary situations that no longer serve your mental health. Believe me, your inner peace is connected with all your aspects of life. I am not saying do not fight for the ones you love, but rather if the ones you love are destroying your inner peace, walk away from their vibe. You do not need to hear it or see it. You may confront it and express what it is that is making you upset at the time, and if the other person is willing to understand, then great. If not, block out the energy.

It was helpful if, the moment I began to think negatively, I got up and drank water. This helped train me into thinking that a source so positive and refreshing can replace negative thoughts. Another strategy is that I would wear a rubber band around my wrist, and once the bubble of inner peace was threatened, I would snap it, so that it would remind me to block away whatever it was that was entering my life. When my anxiety attacks hit, I began to think of how I was living in the now and that the future is yet to come. I cannot control the outcomes of the future, but I can control the present moment. If you reach an impasse where you are stuck about whether or not you should allow the situation or individual into your life, start walking. Start walking away from what doesn't serve you and start walking into the life you want.

The concept of "you only live once" is wrong. We live every day, yet we only die once. Do you really want to live a life that you are not content with? Do you want to live your everyday allowing inanimate objects or beings that serve no purpose into your very existence? I wouldn't, and I don't think you would either. Start by saying no to these things and start by saying yes to what you want that will make you better. Chances are they are probably on the same trip and wouldn't want to do anything that doesn't serve them.

Once I realize my anxiety is acting up, I block the thoughts out by replacing them with more affirming ones. I start counting my blessings and finding grace in all that I do. I know that there are times when, as my mom would say, the devil plays tricks on our minds. This is the time where we need to be the strongest, the time where you need your greatest (I promise you it is within you). The motivation, the power, and the ability to overcome the destruction of your inner peace is found within. Dig deep, find your reason, find the essence of your being and what makes you who you are. Use that energy to channel it to where you are headed and what you have in front of you. Allow that energy to flow from your mind to your heart to the palm of your hand, and when you have it in your grasp, offer it to the world. Allow the world to know that it cannot bring negativity into your life. Block it all out if you have to, so that you can remain a beautiful human being. Block it all out by being kind and gracious to others. Walk away from which that does not serve you into what really does. Listen to your gut; it is your best giver of advice. Listen to your heart; it is the beating reason. Do not stop at just mediocre but get great.

I stop myself when I get into my little zone, and when I do, I take a breather. I allow myself to experience what it is I need to experience and then keep walking about my day. If I say I am great, then I walk in those words. Too many times I have let my anxiety and outer negativity get the best of me, which always led to me destroying others' inner peace. I never wanted that, and I don't think I will ever allow myself to get to that point again. If you know your inner peace is being destroyed, step away for a little while and rebuild. This is where development enters into your life.

Ready, set, action: develop.

The section on blocking and walking was short for a reason. I wanted to give you an insight into my life and how I stopped, adjusted, and reshaped. Stop all from entering your life that doesn't work for you. You are now ready to develop into what you need to be. The truth is that you have been developing this whole time without even noticing. We do things, small things (steps, if you want to call them that) that help us move forward into becoming what we need to be. We are one person one year and the next we are what our experiences made us to be. We develop.

215

You may think that change is your enemy, but it is one of the best things to happen to any of us. As a race, homo sapiens have been known to develop to change the course of our lives. Where we were 20 years ago and where we are today are two different worlds. Everything has changed, nothing is the same anymore, and this isn't a bad thing. You can even consider the mentalities our parents grew up with; they have changed too. This is development. Now whether it is good or bad development depends on what we do that changes the outcome. Sometimes these outcomes better our inner peace, and at times, deconstruct what we have built.

Developing your inner peace and abundance takes all that I have mentioned before and more. In order to develop you must realize that change is on its way. Ask yourself, "Why is it that I need to develop, and what is it that needs development?" Half the time the answer is staring us dead in the eye, but we stay blind to the obvious. If you believe that the current situation is not allowing you to remain at peace, begin development. Start developing your mind into accepting that you need peace and that you must accept this new change.

Half the time we become comfortable with the chaos surrounding us thinking that its part of peace. It really isn't. We have all been there. I've felt comfort and mistaken chaos for peace; it became the norm. The moment you start developing away from this chaos, you start realizing that it was never peace. Peaceful interactions do not come from a place of anger or hatred but rather from a place of love. This is important to keep in mind when you are dealing with any type of 'situationship' or relationship that you are involved in.

As we move forward, we tend to look back at what made us or broke us. I for one am scared of my old self, the angry me.

There was a time when I was ruthless, and my heart had no patience for love or room for peace. I kept everyone at a distance including my emotions and thoughts, making me super robotic. I had no emotions towards anything or anyone, and when it came to anything that didn't go my way, I would black out from anger. I didn't care how things came about; as long as they were in my favor, I was solid. Was this a great way to live? Now that I've developed into a different human being who understands change, it isn't. I'm still scared of that version of myself because I know how dark my energy was and how beaten my peace was.

It's weird to say, after all this time and everything that I have gone through, that I am achieving more peace than I had before 2011. One thing that stands out to me is the time spent and the road traveled. This created more than just an experience for me; the tuition came at the expense of my time. I began to learn how to cope with my downfalls and those around me. Not everyone can be treated the same or have the same relationship with you.

Developing came in stages, as it will for you. It isn't that you wake up one day and realize that you now have inner peace. No. It comes in stages, as your mind builds strength and the other aspects of your life follow suit. There really are no set steps or standards that would make developing your inner peace easier. As you begin to develop a sense of what you need to do to be at peace, you will develop and identify what isn't working for you, while you reshape, adjust, and block. It may take a year, or it may take a month. Developing your inner peace happens at your own pace. It's important that you do not look at your friends or family members and compare your life to theirs. This will only bring chaos into your life, and that isn't healthy.

If the universe asks, it shall receive.

You must have faith in something that helps you push forward. Do you believe that things happen for a reason? Maybe they do or maybe they don't, but if the universe asks, it shall receive. Allow the universe to help you with the construction of your inner peace. If at one point you feel as if the universe is removing toxic people from your life or removing you from toxic situations, let it happen. Allow the magic in your life to happen and don't fight it. Chances are the person you have been fighting to keep in your life was meant to leave a lot earlier. Allow the things you have been holding to walk away if they need to, and those that are meant to stay to stay put.

Do not force your mind into places it does not belong. Be kind to your mind at all times, for it is the hardest-working character within you. If your mind is not at peace, an 8-hour sleep will not give you rest. When you're building your inner peace, you will also have a day or two that won't be fair to you. This unfairness may include some of the roughest times you encounter, times which take so much from you. Don't be alarmed, because the rain doesn't last forever, and the good times will soon be around the corner.

You must weather the storm when working on yourself. Whether you are in the first couple of stages of your build or the last, you must realize that not all goes to plan. The difficulties set in the road do not come to destroy you but rather to show your hidden control. I guarantee that if you begin to reflect on your life, you will realize that whenever you are placed in a corner, you push your way out of it and become great again.

218

When I started renovating my condo, I assessed the damage, reshaping the entire layout, adjust my timelines for any fork in the road, blocking out all the negative energy that didn't serve me at the time, and developing/executing my plan. Things happened along the way that stopped both my physical and mental being: my breakup started, my brother's court case finished, and my work started becoming at risk. I even brought the Cadillac down to a show every Thursday, so that my dad and I could spend more time together.

These were all things that were placed in the road for me to deal with, and at one point, it absolutely destroyed me. I felt that no one could help me, and I felt the absolute need of loneliness. I was hitting my depression again, and my anxiety was at an all-time high. I was dying inside, and my inner peace was on the brink of extinction. I did not know how I was going to come up with the time, effort, and money that my tenant took from me. I did not know how I was going to deal with my breakup or how to possibly fight for the girl that I was no longer with. What were my next steps? How was I going to fix my job and put in better numbers while I was dealing with organizing my life? The thing is that when we look for the answers we need, we don't find them. Instead, they somehow make their way to us through the days that we spend developing into better human beings. You have to let go and let destiny work its magic.

Develop the need to be surrounded by one person: yourself. The independence you offer yourself will always play in your favor if you build that inner peace. You will soon be able to count on yourself, trust yourself, depend on only yourself, and most importantly love yourself. The ability to switch from living a dependent life to an independent one can only come from your ability to change. Causing this development will not hurt you, but rather will help you move ahead.

Learning new ways to create your inner peace is also part of the path you need to take to become yourself again. We all have experienced inner peace; we lose it along the way. Attain it again, learn to live with it again. I think one of the biggest hurdles we go through is allowing life to play itself out. Believe in the fact that you are developing and in a constant path of development and change. We are not the same people we were last year, and we won't be next year. However, if we allow chaos to enter our lives, we will become worse.

Be understanding of everything that enters into your world, as it all has a purpose. Developing is also understanding what belongs and what doesn't. If it doesn't, you've been able to take a lesson out of it and use it for your experience. If it does, your life only gets better. Do not be afraid of the inevitable change. Humans are meant to develop. It is up to you as to how you want to create your inner peace.

Exit Thoughts

It is important to realize what we are surrounded by what causes either chaos or peace. We sometimes live our days without paying any attention to the surroundings, but as mentioned in Chapter 2, we need to stop and smell the flowers. When I started writing this chapter, I did not think it would be one of the longest; it just goes to show you that peace comes from so much. There is still so much I haven't been able to write or point out regarding how I became the human that I am today.

When I started writing I really wanted to find more peace in my life. I knew that I was able to communicate my past experiences and what they had taught me, in hopes that some of it might work for others. If I bored you, I apologize. If I made you cry, I apologize. But if I made you feel any type of emotion, then I believe we have connected.

I truly hope that we all can find the inner peace we are looking for in our lives. Whether it is that you are mentally or physically at peace, we all need it. My exit thoughts are a little different for this chapter, as it touches on one of the most important subjects. I left peace for the end of the book for multiple reasons, as it ties together the first 9 chapters. I hope that you find what you are looking for and that you find the peace you require.

If you choose to, know that forgiving without an apology holds so much power. The ability to control your mind with what you want and how you live is a type of peace. Allow your inner peace to showcase love and be surrounded by love, because love is the cure to all chaos. I pray that you realize (through my trials and tribulations) that inner peace is still attainable. If you surround yourself with peaceful individuals, you will become one of them. If you surround yourself will chaos, you become that. The road you have traveled might have not been easy, but I promise you, you've got this. Continue on with whatever it is you are dealing with, and if adjusting, reshaping, blocking/walking, and developing helps, then for your sake I am thankful.

I aim to build a connection, and even though we may never know each other, I hope you realize that the world is built on love. If you somehow attain this inner peace, show it to someone who is at war with themselves. Helping someone achieve peace will be rewarding. When we depart this world, all we have is our legacy. Give the world your all and don't shy away from wearing your heart on your sleeve. The world needs more of you and less hatred because hatred is the root of all chaos. Allow yourself to become the person you need to be. Remember that you need rain for rainbows.

I hope I have been able to help. If not, then I apologize. Write me, and maybe we can have a conversation.

CHAPTER 11

Domino Effect: The Last Straw

What is it that determines our fate or our last option? I think it is all the experiences that took place beforehand. Right up until now, we have always had the opportunity to make choices that have impacted our lives in so many ways. Now is when you begin to realize that it has all played out to your benefit and caused you to become who you are today. One brick after the other, your foundation is built without your awareness. This indicates the positive domino effect that you have been waiting for. The dominos are falling in line for your destiny.

Have you had faith this whole time that it will all work out, or have you just been shooting for the stars and aiming for the moon? Half the time we start with daily activities without realizing that with every hour that passes, we get closer to attaining our goals. Be very aware of your actions, for they will become future results.

I left this chapter till the end because I really wanted to connect the earlier writings. I wanted to take the "Hustle" chapter and incorporate that with the "Risk," chapter along with "As You Are, You Are Beautiful." There's a concrete connection to everything that I have written, and I will spend time to explain it. This is probably going to be the most detailed chapter, and I plan to connect with you emotionally and on a soul level. I believe that, through my trauma and everything that I have experienced, a lesson can be learnt.

It is currently 1:30 a.m. on a Friday night in March. I am in a totally vulnerable state of mind, and I believe that this is the perfect time for me to write. I am sitting in my home office with the lights off after a long day of working and having my gears turned. I live alone, hence all I hear is the sound of the street traffic coming from outside my balcony. It is crazy to say this, but all I remember and feel in this very instance is peace. I don't think I mentioned it, but night is when I feel that I am at peace and that I am the happiest. It is when the world stops for a few hours. I am tempted to stop writing and go to sleep, but that wouldn't be the right thing to do. I am also conflicted with how to go about this, but what better way to spill my heart out than with communication from my mind through my fingers.

So here goes nothing.

Now that you have gotten an idea of what my surroundings are like and how I am feeling, I hope you understand what I am about to say. I have never felt more alive. I am beginning to realize that life isn't about what it makes of you but rather what you make of it. I wrote in my previous chapters that you need to hustle out of the reality that you are in, and I truly meant that. My reality has been changing; whether it was my breakups, relationships, or even my career, it was forever changing. My hustle changed my reality, so that I can understand what is going on and I can control it. After so many years of the traumatic experiences that life has thrown at me, I am finally beginning to understand why it has all happened.

If you do not see the reason things are happening now, know that it somehow will work out, and you will eventually know the reason. Having faith in destiny is key to realizing that it will all fall in place for you. Do not have faith without hard work though. For your destiny to play its role, you must hustle so that you can fall in line with what is meant for you.

Once when I was supposed to fly out of Lebanon and back to Canada, the airports had canceled their flights to France. I was confused, but somehow, I had rebooked my flight to Italy, and then to Germany, which eventually flew me to Toronto. When I got to Germany, I remember being so lost that I felt very small in a large world. I continued to believe that no matter what happened, I was going to hustle my way out of it. My risk was that would I miss my flight or become lost.

When you are hustling your way out of the reality you are living into the reality you want, you tend to risk a lot of things, things that may be temporary, but the risk you take will move you to a more successful position in life. You also become more in control of your life and start to heal all the salted wounds. Isn't that beautiful? Do you think you can find the beauty in that? What about hustling your way into your reality while recovering from your pain and trauma is not beautiful?

Don't be ashamed of telling yourself, before you even speak aloud, that your perfection lies in the brief imperfections in your life. Say it with your chest for everyone to hear and understand. More important, realize that it's okay to hustle your healing.

How is it all connected?

Slowly but surely, you will see that this chapter sums up all that I have written about previously. It takes into consideration the hustle, the pain, the communication, the beauty, and the trauma and gives you a way to look at my story. I really want you to understand me and my background, so that you can realize that you're not alone or that there are people suffering who don't show it.

I want you to also become cognisant of the fact that we all have a story, and although we may not show it, some of us are suffering in ways that we may not understand. Suffering and pain sometimes find their way into the world through smiles and laughs. Sometimes those who are going through it are dealing with it by showing extra care and love to others, while deep down they are aching for someone to do the same.

We say that we need to consider the person that we are talking to, because as we do not know what they have gone through, but do we really follow that rule?

I find most of us say things, but they drift away on the wind. So, what can allow us to follow through with our word? It is emotional intelligence and compassion (or understanding empathy). These two ideas apply to almost any case, and if understood correctly, can help to change our interactions. We need to realize that our daily activities are tied into every thought, word, emotion, and all 5 senses. We can understand that how we interact with others will change our lives.

As a race we need to develop the method of understanding. We mustn't judge what we see but rather question the reason behind the actions. At times, people act from a reason deep within, one that they have not yet spoken about. We only see the results of this pain or trauma, and if we're lucky, we see those who hide it very well. Please, I urge you, do not judge a book by its cover, for the pages written in that book are stories by different authors and events in that person's life.

While writing this book over the last 4 years, I have put in 90% of the work in the last 4 months (from the beginning of 2021 to March). I had spent the last 4 years developing and risking myself to the world to grow. This was not an intentional act but rather life taking its course Post-January I had gone through a slew of emotions at times that allowed me to write, nights spent on my laptop writing while the world was asleep, and nights where I ended up imploring my heart to sleep. I intended to do one thing, and that was to feel and embrace all my emotions throughout. I kept to myself this time around and didn't really show the weak side of myself to anyone. Not that I didn't want to seem fragile, but rather because I wanted to experience that vulnerability and to realize where I don't want to be, and to build on that. I realized that I was doing what I wrote about in 2016 and 2017, such as hustling my way out of the reality, taking control, and the other concepts.

When life gives you lemons, make lemonade.

Here's what I mean.

Life sometimes will throw wrenches in your gears to stop or halt production of whatever positivity you are developing. You need to realize that the emotions developed from this bump in the road are life's way of developing your strong suit. After all, your best stories are from life's harshest trials. You will go through your ranks of pain and then later create your ways of getting over things or developing your ways of healing. This creates a strong asset of self-reliance. Reshaping your mind to this new mentality is not easy and will take some effort. You will soon begin to look at the cup as half full rather than half empty. Sometimes, you'll need to look at the cup as just a cup, but when you are hustling your way into the reality you want, you must look at what voids you can fill in a positive way. So, when life gives you lemons, you make lemonade and then figure out how to sell drinks. It's easier said than done, but you must evolve to survive.

I spoke about beauty and how we are all unique. We tend to forget that the beauty comes from the life we live, and that even though we may act in an ugly manner at times, our core nature was once the same. Think about it: we were all once children, being raised by parents who saw the innocence in us. I sincerely believe that that innocence still exists, and that if we dig deep, we will find it. Somewhere along the line we began to grow and change and adapt to new ways, placing walls in our house of vulnerability.

We develop and somehow become the beauty that we choose. You have developed into the human you are today, and that beauty itself is beautifully accepted. You are your own ray of sunshine, and no one can ever take that away from you. Your capabilities may differ from the next person, but that does not mean that you are not able to do all that you want. Experiences help us learn and allow us to develop the beauty within us.

Have you not been able to see the beauty in you, or the fact that you are unique, created to be 1 of 1?

Life isn't easy, and living it is even harder. You get hit with problems, situations, and issues that you had never expected or knew how to deal with. This is the building block that will help you move forward. Is this an ugly trait? Not at all. An old friend of mine used to say, "Life is beautiful," and I thought she was being overly positive. I now understand that phrase, some 14 years later. Life is how you want to look at it, and even though the trauma and darkness you have encountered may have been able to alter that image, it still has hidden beauty.

This is the same concept that I spoke about in the "keeping the peace" chapter. You will be bombarded by issues and things that you have no experience with, but the beauty is that you learn and are able to come out of it stronger. You are beautiful in everything you do. Many other people realize that, too, but they just don't say it. Communication has been lost over the years, even though access to technology is easier.

That's a weird way of thinking about it, huh? We now are closer but further apart than ever before.

Those who want to praise you don't do so out of fear of ego. Those who don't have any positive feedback see all your moves, hence allowing hate to grow. I have seen family members utter words of hate, so don't feel as if you are alone. The phrase "if you don't have anything good to say, don't say anything at all" is a good one.

If you are reading and have reached this far, I'm proud of you.

Please celebrate your circle of friends; celebrate their wins as if they were your own. Even if you are not winning now, your time will come, and they, too, will soon praise you. Allow yourself to get into the mentality of appreciating the beauty around you, because who you are is an exact derivative of those closest to you. Regarding "as you are, you are beautiful," I wrote about keeping what makes you beautiful and what makes you, you. Conforming to society's norms isn't something that should be done or even taken into consideration. Changing who you are shouldn't even be an option.

I wrote that 2016 through 2017, and I didn't change much of it in 2021. I believed in everything I said. There was a time that I did not follow through with it, though, and I started to change myself while in a relationship, which was a very unhealthy way of life. I lost myself, and I honestly would never do it again. It isn't healthy (you don't need a therapist to tell you this) to change who you are for anyone or anything.

Do not make permanent decisions in temporary situations as it will destroy you in the long run, regardless of where you are in life. I want you to look at yourself in a very positive manner, thinking that you are the catch of a lifetime. However, do know that it comes with responsibility. You need to be human and allow yourself to go through all the emotions necessary to live.

We live our days without realizing that the end is death. We all will die one day, and not to sound like a pessimist, but do you really want to go on living, not considering yourself as an amazing human being? You are one of one, there is no other like you, not even a twin. Believe it or not, you are special, if not to Person A, then to Person B, and that is important. You could be the reason someone is fighting to live another day or the reason someone is happy.

I hope I have helped you in some way. Things haven't been normal lately, not for any of us (as I think we can agree). I have been taking a risk with everything that I have shared. Vulnerability is not weakness; it involves the ability to realize risk and reward. I may see myself from one view and others may see me in another. The point is that risk is defined as you choose, and reward is subjective, based on the outcome. Every time I speak, I want the truth to come out. It's the only real thing that allows you to see me for what I really am.

Is beauty worth the risk?

Risk comes in different shapes and forms, and as I'm sure as you can tell, my life has been encompassed by risk. To be fair, I believe we experience this on a daily, and your life may be filled with risk too. Whether it was immediate risk or risk that became clear later, I managed to be part of that timeline. A result of risk is the possibility of regret. Do I regret anything? I don't believe so.

I had a conversation with my dad once, and I might have touched on this in the previous chapters, but I will reiterate. He was reflecting and told me that the decisions he made 'back in the day' weren't the best ones. Had he known the result things would have been totally different. My answer wasn't comforting but rather my opinion. I said, "If you thought the decisions you made at that time were the right ones, then they were worth the risk, and regret is off the table." Life is a gamble, and the results are about how you play it. Sometimes life gives odds that are not in your favor, and the only guarantee we have in life is death. So, why not live now?

My father had grown up in an era where men put food on the table. If, as the man of the house, he had to starve so that his kids could eat, that was just the responsibility he took on. I have seen my father take risks in his life, and the largest risk he took was coming to Canada for a better life. I can see where the regret lies in his heart, however, no one really knew the outcome of such a risky move. This regret comes from a lifetime of decision-making, and I totally understand it.

You mustn't allow fear to consume you when you want to risk it all. Think and make calculated decisions, but at the same time realize that if the circumstances do not play out in your favor, you have not failed. One setback could be your greatest comeback, and that is the standard I want you to embrace.

You really tend to fight your way out of a corner once you have no options. The risk then becomes your only option, and you are left to fend for any outcome it gives you. When I left for Lebanon, I realized that the risk I needed to take was to become part of the people in any way possible. I slowly started learning the lingo, the physical demeanor, the ability to haggle and to act like the local people, and before I knew it, I began to realize that my risk was working out. What I didn't realize was that the great outcome was also hiding a disadvantage. I was beginning to forget the ways of my Canadian heritage and life that I had built in Toronto. Even though I was born in Lebanon, and my bloodline is Lebanese, Canada is home, and it's where I am from. This is where I began to look at the man in the mirror and really wanted to start making a change.

Whose reflection is this?

I didn't want to become a different human being but to become adaptable. Part of risking my freedom and vulnerability in Lebanon was learning to change my self-image. Mind you, my brother had just passed away in my arms, I had just fled the country over safety concerns, my mother was still in pain, my father was suffering on his own, and everyone and their mother wanted to know what happened back in Toronto. So, I was confused ... lost to say the least. That's a lot for a 21-year-old to handle. Until then, the closest I had been to stress was failing a pop-up quiz or my computer breaking down during an exam.

It hurts every time I think about what I have gone through and have yet to understand. I remember thinking that I needed to get better, and till this day I have the same thoughts in all my reflections. Whether my mirror is fogged or not, I tend to see the ability to change. I couldn't blame anyone but myself; who else was to take blame for what happened in my life?

Are we truly a product of our environment, or are we what we allow our environment to make us?

Our surroundings don't have the upper hand. The circumstances which surround our lives can only bring us to greatness or take us from it. You have control over that, and if you can take control of your present, the future is yours. (Side note: I used to hate showing my vulnerability or being the nice guy. It always made me think people would view me as weak. But if I break my personality down and take away that trait, I am someone like the rest.) I have a conscience, empathy, and an intuition like no other. My creativity alone will create paths for life, as well as my appreciation for the little things and my understanding for others' pain. Take away that trait, the trait of my reflection, and it takes me away from the world. My reflection is the one that stares back at me, and the one that you may view as weak, but it's me. It's beautiful.

Think about that one single trait that makes you who you are, and now imagine it being taken away. Who would you be? Do you want to be like the rest, or do you want your reflection, to be that 1 of 1?

Shape your world with control.

The thing I hate most in life is not being in control, but somehow, knowing that I can let life take its course brings comfort. I like being in control; it's the dominant side of me. But I know that when it's time to delegate, I can. Every situation or relationship is like a business, and sometimes it's best to let those who can perform amazingly in certain areas do just that.

My life has been the exact result of the 5 fingers of control. With the ability to control my mindset, my respect, my ability to learn how to accept blame without caring for opinions, and loving people, I know that I can somehow control my mentality. I am not one to control people or to have the mindset that I need to control the individuals around me, but I do believe that I need to be in control of my own mind.

With everything that has been happening in our lives, our anxiety and overthinking has been at an all-time high. That's why I really was focusing on controlling the mind. The thoughts that may come to mind that are chaotic or not in our favor must not linger long enough to cause damage. (Side note: I am finding it relatively difficult to end this book with this chapter. Thinking I should go back and add more ... add more to the pages and chapters. I can now reflect on and give my opinion with all the growth I have recently gone through. Feeling nice ... might add more later. Who knows?)

Thinking about how I chose to take control of my life and how it all played out, I think it worked to my benefit. That's me controlling my outlook on things with the intent of being okay with the losses I have been dealt. Relatively speaking, of course, these losses were catastrophic and life-altering. I don't think I was ever able to love again as I did in 2019. I never thought in a million years that I would be able to settle in a country so unknowingly and suddenly. I sometimes look at the past 10 years and think that life could have been so different had that night not taken place. Along the way, I have gained new friends, new insights, new thought process, and, more importantly, the ability to find areas in my heart that I did not know existed. I lost my brother, and I will forever mourn his loss. He will forever be my brother. I will continuously speak of him as if he is still here with us, but with the darkness that arrived in my life that day, I was somehow able to find happiness again.

It may be incomplete happiness, but it's happiness none the less.

Taking control was one thing but knowing when to walk away from certain situations was another. After Shadi's absence I started holding grudges against those who I felt did my family wrong. What I thought I was doing was right turned out to be wrong. I held a grudge against a cousin of mine for a situation prior Shadi's death, and it wasn't till years later that I forgave him. I decided I needed to walk away from that individual back then, but all I was doing was walking right into my hurt. Sometimes without realizing it we walk away not from those who injure us, but into our injury itself. We don't know it at the time, and it could disguise itself as the right option, but it isn't.

My latest love told me that holding a grudge does me no good, and it only creates more pain in my life. She was right. (God, do I hate to admit she was right. Ha!) When I forgave my cousin, I did it with no apology. I was just tired of playing into my pain that had caused me to distance myself from family due to their mistake at the time.

At some point you realize that you need to stop and know when to walk away from the pain. Grabbing onto that pain does you no good. (If you disagree with me, soon you will soon realize it for yourself.) Knowing this, I can also say that if you are going holding grudges or pain, go through it. Do not stop until you know that you are ready to let go. There is no timeline but rather a date "when you are ready" to let go and move on.

We are all different and our lives reflect different journeys. When I wrote "The Emergency Button," I was in my feelings about my recent circumstances, and somehow all my previous walkaways came back to mind. After writing it, I realized that I had recently implemented the same method in my life, the 'stop and go' methodology. I knew it was time that to let go of lingering situations, but never would I have thought that I would then be okay. Some situations come back to mind often, and even though I let go of them, I constantly think about them. My everyday process is thinking about the people or events involved in those situations (as in "Keeping the Peace").

I can hear you.

Most of us leave situations because they either no longer serve us or because they threaten our peace. What we don't realize is that much of this is due to poor communication. Many of the world's problems and arguments could be solved if the ego and pride were in check. Most of my relationships had misunderstandings that were sometimes unresolved and were the results of the two. One person had an ego or pride that they couldn't let go, and it was awful to see it crumble.

We have all been there, and I think that if we truly dig deep, we'll realize that we can work on our own communication. In these times, it is vital that we talk out the emotions that we have been holding back. Believe it or not, it also could be the thing that is preventing you from moving forward with your life. Holding in the words that you need to express will do you so much more harm than good. Speaking up or communicating comes with trust, and it could be hard to find someone to talk to, but you must find a way to communicate with yourself.

Is it really a 'you only live once' mentality?

For years I have had the mentality of 'here today, gone tomorrow.' I have a very simple rule: I don't go to bed angry or upset with anyone or anything. This stems from the fact that I have realized how precious life is, and that no problem is large enough that it cannot be solved. We really can fix our problems before it is too late; however, the pride within us that is disguised by anger won't let us. I guess my biggest regret is not fixing all the issues I had with my brother. It really does hurt my heart; hence, I don't ever want to leave any unattended issues before bed.

When I wrote the chapter "Can You Hear Me?" I wanted to understand the faults in all my relationships. I wanted to write about the basis of all relationship breaks that have either come my way or that I have been witness to. I found that it started with one's own self. The words that we communicate on the daily, whether to other people or to ourselves, is the determining factor.

Along with the thoughts that come into our minds, our only reality is created when we speak. The more negativity spoken, the more the energy you draw to those words. If you speak with positive reinforcement, you slowly begin to change your vibe. I realized a flaw of mine along the way, which was that I cuss too much. Noting that I was usually uttering the 'F-word' every few sentences, I began to become disgusted. I would even be very harsh on myself, and that would lead me to develop self-confidence issues. I not only saw this in myself, but I noticed how everyone around me was moving. Friends or acquaintances who were very soft spoken were peaceful. They might have not been on the inside, but the words that they projected were slowly changing their vibe.

Can I communicate pain?

Maybe you can. Maybe you shouldn't. Maybe you need to forgive without apology those who caused you pain. We feel, and that makes us human. Allow your emotional intelligence to shine through when you are feeling the pain. If you have been wounded, allow your wounds to turn into scars that you wear ever so bravely. Do not allow your past wounds to dictate the hardness of your heart. Rather love again and allow the softness of your heart to beat through into the world. Pain only lasts if we want it to, and if we continuously communicate this pain, we will always be placing ourselves in this bubble of toxic remembrance. Ever remember a time when you thought the pain you were going through was going to last forever? You're probably doing much better and have learnt so much from what you have gone through. That is called resilience, and you, my friend, are a warrior.

All you had to do was let time take time.

The healing process is not the same every time. It really is subjective and will always change according to what you are dealing with in your life. Allow yourself the opportunity to feel the healing as well. It may come in stages, but you will know what lessons you have adopted into your life the moment you start reflecting. Think about the last time your heart or soul experienced pain. Does it still hurt? It may still linger, but you have now learnt to live with the pain.

This learning curve in your life is much better to have than not, and here's why. Lessons are taught through the work on a subject. Throughout your process you might realize that it isn't for you, or rather that what is happening to you is not something you want to keep around. Once you begin realizing what doesn't serve you or what you know has caused you pain, you start to recognize the pain before it even develops. These lessons cannot be taught here, and the only way to ever realize them is to go through them yourself.

Your peace is important.

Living in chaos or pain isn't forever. You may be battling with your inner demons about issues that seem permanent, but that is you conceptualizing the idea of enduring pain. Dealing with how to get out of pain has been explained in the previous chapters. Keeping the peace is one of the most important parts of this book. I was privileged that at the time of my writing I was communicating with the world the inner peace that I was looking for. I was dealing with a very chaotic life and was not able to find my peace with many situations. I was holding onto grudges and pain that were caused years ago and that no longer aided me. I began to learn and adapt to allow forgiveness without apologies; this became my motto for developing peace. I was going through my breakup along with other personal factors at the time and was in a state of pure chaos. This wasn't a fun time, but in the rubble, I found my gem of peace.

We want peace, regardless of the shape or form. We want to be able to perform our daily tasks without disarray entering our lives. With this, we as a race of human beings need to recognize that the want must be genuine. The ability to achieve inner peace and outer peace only comes at the expense of hard work and time. Realize that the effort put in in the short term will come back 10-fold.

Your peace is important to you and to those around you. Allowing yourself to create a peaceful bubble of thoughts or in life will not only reflect the happiness you achieved, but it will also slowly begin to give those around you a sense of security as well.

I hope I didn't confuse you with the idea of cutting off people so that you can develop your inner peace. I am not saying this so that you think I am focusing on the group of people around you. No. Forgoing your group of friends for a minute and focusing on yourself will allow you to develop a quality of friendship and relationships you may have never experienced before. If finding your inner peace will cause you to lose some friendships short-term, know that the friendships you develop once you have reshaped and adjusted your bubble will be high-quality. I think that's what we all want, a place where we can kick it, knowing that everyone around us is at peace, or at least can accept peace in their lives.

Conceptualize your life.

The concepts of adjusting, reshaping, blocking/walking, and developing for peace are ways that worked for me. While writing I realized that I had been following these steps all my life. At times, chaos was imminent; however, my mentality was too. In fact, my life has been like that, and that is all I have ever known: to fight. I am not playing the victim role here, but I am being realistic. Chaos and disturbance have always found me, regardless of where I am and what I am doing. This I see to be part of life, my life. Maybe you can relate?

Sometimes those who are good-hearted find chaos because they want to change the world, not knowing that by doing so, they themselves are developing. Reflecting back, I have sometimes been the one to find chaos and to bring it to a peaceful surrounding. Maybe that's my flaw.

My peace is important; hence I need to begin adjusting to my new mentality of allowing chaos to pass by me while I do nothing about it. I realized that I need to start observing more than reacting. Think of chaos as a person who is passing, and that you have the option to either stop them and talk or watch them go past.

A lot of the times we see the future but disregard the present. The forward-looking may allow us to hope for peace, however the present disruption presents nothing but confusion. This is where it is key that we stop ourselves and adjust, block, and walk. We must adjust our mentality to thinking about the present in this situation rather than the potential of what that person can be. Apply this in your relationships with people you are dealing with day-to-day. Do not think of what this situation can bring you down the line but consider if the disruption of your current peace is worth it. Know that life, although lived every day, will end. Do you want to live your life in hopes of peace or rather act today to achieve happiness?

The Last Straw

The last straw can be picked by you. If you stack your dominos in a correct form without any outside movement, you will achieve the impossible. Remember the previous chapters and know that it's all a domino effect. Planning and organizing your life never went out of fashion, and you may find that you do this continuously, as we are ever building our lives.

Do not worry about other humans' perceptions of your journey. Half the time those judging you are judging themselves for not having the peace or the resilience that you may embody. It's not that it's important that we don't care about the judgment of others but rather that we need to care more about our process of growth. Once you truly start placing the pieces of your life's 'dominos' in a row, you will begin to realize that you have no time for others' opinions or distractions. If you begin to allow these irrelevant thoughts into your life, not only are you taking away from your achievements, but you delay reaching the end goal.

The last straw: do not come to a point where you have had enough. Build and continuously work at maintaining your life to the standard you want. Neither I nor anyone else is capable of dictating how you should or shouldn't live. Do not allow the frustration in you to build up to a point of no return. If there are issues bothering you, speak up about them at that moment rather than allowing them to build, or you will reach your boiling point and inadvertently explode. This may be uncontrollable and will communicate the wrong ideas, if not the wrong self-perception. It's about communication.

We need to work on the little things each day if we are looking to change our lives. Peace, communication, beauty, positivity, a hustle like no other, control, and allowing love to enter our lives are some of the most important features we can create. I urge you to be human with everyone and everything around you. Being empathetic never went out of style. If this is your 'last straw,' I am happy for you. This is your change, your indication of adjusting into a more fulfilling life.

You really are hustling 4 happiness.

I think we all are.

CHAPTER 12

My Final Thoughts

This book has been a thrill. I have experienced and felt so much while writing it. I have also come to so many conclusions in my life that I have shared with you. I truly believe that there is some substance there for everyone. Whether you are dealing with some issue or not, I hope I have been of some help. The timeline for this book was one that I did not expect. I really wasn't anticipating a 4-year writing process. It really wasn't until January of 2021 that I really went through it all and absolutely killed it. I only had 4 chapters written in December of 2020, and even those weren't finished. I started writing in January and was able to write 7 chapters and finally complete the first 4. It's currently April, and I'm writing my final goodbye. After a decade of emotions, heartbreaks, anxiety, depression, stress, unhappiness, and a broken soul, it's time that I allow it all to come to an end so that I can move on.

Along the way, I have met so many people and seen so many faces that have impacted my life in ways I could have never imagined. The fact is that without those experiences, I wouldn't have been able to bring this book to life. I think we can all agree that our lives are impacted by the events that occur around us or within us. The effects don't necessarily hit right away, but eventually we find the lessons.

During my writing period of the last four to five years, I have noticed that life really has no mercy regarding time. The moments turn into memories, and the memories become stored in your mind, and life really becomes one for the books. I have experienced a few Kodak moments in the last decade, and I can tell you that I have cherished them all. I have learnt from all those around me regardless of the lesson. Now that I look back at it, I am beginning to really feel the effects of all the hardships I have gone through. Maybe this is time for you to reflect on the last decade of your life and write down what you appreciate.

What have you learned?

I found that I really was able to speak to you when I was at my most defenceless. Regardless of whether it was my mind, my heart, or my soul that was in a state of vulnerability, I was able to come to you in my truest form. To be honest, I didn't want to write in any other way. I felt that I'd be cheating you. I have been able to write my emotions and my truest of thoughts about all that has happened. Whether they were good or bad, I hope I have come across as truthful. I wanted you to feel the emotions in the words that I wrote, and by writing in a highly emotional state, I hope I achieved that. I don't want you to feel sympathy towards my journey but rather a state of understanding.

We all experience trauma and issues that we don't necessarily speak about. The embodiment of this stress is what is slowly eating at our souls since we don't really come out and say much. As a man, it took me almost 11 years to book a session with a therapist about issues that I have yet to solve. So, I hope you realize you are not alone. Therapy did one thing for me that I was not able to do before, which is to speak with someone about my issues from an outsider's perspective that offered no judgement whatsoever. I was not a bad person, and neither was I a great human being. I was simply human.

The more we don't communicate about what is happening in our lives, the more we are closed off to ourselves. We take away from the life we are living by not communicating with others and more importantly by not communicating with ourselves. Over the last decade I have encountered individuals who have not been able to speak to about the truth that has been hiding deep within. I guess coming to terms, at times, is a lot harder than rushing away from the responsibility and consequences.

Being able to experience the different nations of both Canada and Lebanon also brought me a new perspective on life. This was a lesson that I could not have anticipated or paid for even if I wanted to. The ability to allow things to flow and to allow your destiny to unfold at its pace was not one that I was privy to. Until this day, I sometimes find myself forcing things rather than allowing them to occur naturally. Do not confuse this with control or anything that I wrote about in the chapter on control, as this is a forceful destination.

Have you reflected recently?

In the recent months I have been thinking about what has happened over the last year and more importantly the impact my brother's absence. It has been very pot-holed but, somehow, I have written this book, and I am still alive. The absence of my brother Shadi has left a hole in all our hearts. It has changed us, it has molded us, it has allowed us to become empathetic, it has beaten us, and it has made us stronger. This wasn't something I knew would be the outcome. I never thought I'd make it out alive after 2011. I didn't even think I would make it to 2020, let alone the years that passed by.

We learned to hide pain behind smiles for everyone to see. Maybe that wasn't the way to go about things, but the events of that time required us to act in certain ways. With my brother's absence, I found that I began to understand how fragile life can be and started implementing that in my daily routine. It wasn't until later that I realized that not everyone understands this concept, and that's okay. This last chapter is about my communication with you, about my thoughts on the whole ordeal, more than anything. I was able to understand that not everyone understood my pain or how appreciative I was for life. I may have gone about a few things in the wrong way, but at the end, the lesson learnt was greater than the pain felt. A lot of people can be 'in the know' of what happened, but to understand the pain or emotion you are going through, they'd have to experience it themselves.

If you have suffered any type of trauma that has changed your views on life, it's okay. I hope that in time it becomes a view of love and tolerant acceptance. It hasn't beat you, by the way, and it never will. The situation you are in (or were in or may even be in in the future) will not beat you. My biggest regret is not seeing how strong I am. This isn't my weakness but my blindness, and it could very well be yours. In the moment, you probably didn't think you could get through it, because all you were focused on was the pain. That adrenaline rush really is hard to let go of to focus on anything else. Once things calm down, relax your mind, and think about how you're going to come out of this. If you need to, think about my situation. If I was able to get out of all my misery and trauma, you can too.

There really is no stopping any of us from becoming great, other than the mindset we place ourselves in. If you can change your mentality, you'll be able to change your life. This doesn't just start with your thinking, but it also includes the way you speak. If your speech is full of hate or words that do not utter love, your whole vibe changes. It might be hard dealing with a change of this sort, but you can do it. I don't know you, but I believe that you can change your life for the better. Take it from someone who has been at his lowest and has reached a high point in his life: it can all change in the blink of an eye. You can start living out your best days today and the next minute be hit with a tragedy. In all of this, I ask that you remain humble, not so that you are labeled that way but so you are humble towards life. The ability to appreciate life for the good and the bad is a trait you can achieve.

I have also learned to tell the difference between hate and love, and I have very little space in my heart for hate. I truly believe that love trumps all, and it's the reason I love so hard. Somehow it all goes back to January 24, 2011, the reason behind everything that I feel. Life is precious and at the same time so valuable; we tend to forget its worth. I have gone through all the emotions that the world has thrown at me, and it has all lead me to the topic of love. My views on this may differ from yours, but it really can change the world. Never would I have thought that one word can hold this much importance or be this heavy on one's soul. But the solution to all the anger and hatred in your life or in this world can be solved by one simple 4-letter word. Isn't that crazy?

It is the love of oneself that can create love amongst others. This love must be created and developed by your own body, and the acceptance of your life comes from gratitude. I never knew the power of the love I can give someone, until I was able to find the love that I gave myself. With this comes the ability to be certain beyond measure of your love towards others.

At one point in 2020, I was asked, "Why/how are you so certain of me and us?" It never really dawned on me that my communication of love towards myself was so immense that I had the ability to make room for so much more love towards another person. Since my mentality about myself was certain, I was able to become certain about this person in ways that I never thought possible, and that was the power of my love towards them. It wasn't in material items or in the words uttered, but in the certainty of the future.

Individuals like us can be blind to the potential we have as human beings. Confusion only rests in the misery that does not know love. It is my opinion that love once experienced can be the root of all success and forever happiness. If you have experienced love with anyone and have been in love, you must know that you forgive every situation you are in for the good of love and life.

What is it that creates love?

I believe it to be the time, effort, and life spent creating memories that can last a lifetime. I found that the choice of loving or being loved really is within me to give or take. The ability to become vulnerable so that one can embrace the love they have and be able to give it to others is a strong trait. You really must not allow your past love to interfere with your present. The current moment you live in is a gift given to you every morning. It is then that you define a space of your own.

Love can heal damaged souls. It can place a smile back on someone's face. This love isn't romantic love, but rather love in its entirety, love from a parent, from a friend, from a pet. I want you to keep an open mind. Love can be in any shape or form. I know you have experienced love at some point. Do you recall the joy you felt or the way your heartbeat raced, knowing that you were in love or rather loved by someone? It's that high that we all chase, whether we want to show it or not.

Life isn't short; life is a long journey, and we are living to make it worthwhile. Each day, you can choose to show love or accept hatred into your life. Either way you are living, but with one, you will always be winning.

Emotional Intelligence

At times we cannot control our emotions, yet we can focus on negative thoughts more than anything. As an overthinker and a person who has anxiety, the life of living in fear isn't guaranteed. I tend to find that we want to focus on the 'what ifs' of the future rather than 'what nows' of the present. The problem lies within our minds, and mental health issues are only now being recognized. It took a pandemic for the topic of mental health to become a serious issue.

As a Middle Eastern man, I'm not encouraged to go and speak with someone about getting over trauma. Our culture doesn't really have that trait. Control of your emotions comes from the ability to snap back into reality. What the future holds for us is unknowable, and there is no guarantee that any situation or relationship will work out in anyone's favor. I mentioned before that the choice to be happy or filled with misery lies within me, and so does the choice of resilience or giving up. The moment you're able to wake up every day is the moment your decision comes into action. Your ability to choose your happiness or sadness determines the rest of your day, and it may be hard, but taking one step at a time is the key to this strategy. The small steps during your day make all the difference in the end.

Emotions can really be the bearers of bad news in our lives. The moment we lose control of these feelings or thoughts, we begin regressing. It's not the control of the feelings that cause the regression but rather the outcome of what these thoughts do to us. Life will play its role in your timeline, and you will begin to see that when you become more aware of its implications. You must realize, however, that it really is a constant fight to stay afloat. I have begun to realize that my fight usually starts in the morning and continues during the day. Unresolved trauma usually can do this, but it's okay, and know if you are willing to get help or to move on with your life, you're already winning.

The first step toward change is realizing that the change is needed. It's important to be aware of what is wrong and where you need to be. Self-awareness is key, and I want you to be hawk-eyed during your transition into the great human being you're meant to be. Reflect on what is wrong and start thinking about the process to correct this. If you can identify where things have gone south, then, my friend, you are on the path of success. Most of us get blinded by the process and get frustrated trying to understand what went wrong (in any situation). The reflection phase is most helpful. Regardless of who comes to our aid (friends or life), if the aid is there, we are beginning to heal.

In March and April (while writing this book), my bubble of peace was consumed by chaos, chaos that I had allowed into my life inadvertently and had kept there for a few days. I had a conversation with a friend regarding my bubble of peace being infiltrated and how my vibe was off. She said that I knew what was happening, and the fact that I was knowledgeable enough to realize that my peace was altered was my first step to healing. Once my anger blew off, I knew right away what had caused the introduction of this chaos in my life. Taking some time was all I really needed to do to brush this all out of my system. I began to get rid of this blind anger day by day, getting back into reality, and slowly but surely, I was able to get back to my space of peace. This may not work for you, or it may, however I can't tell you what to do. This whole book has been meant to help those around me and those I have not yet met or will probably never meet.

My life hasn't been one that you can call normal, and neither do I ever expect it to be. I have come to terms with that, and I truly believe that, even though I wish things could have been different, they'll never be. This isn't a sympathy plea and never will be. This is more of a truthful beginning to a future of beautiful and peaceful indulgence. I come with baggage, baggage that not a lot of people can handle and fluctuating emotions that people hate. I have become very honest with myself regarding what and where I am in my life. One thing that we can all begin to do that can help us recognize the beauty within us is to be truthful about who we are. If we can only accept the flaws and the imperfections there along the way, we can truly begin to embrace the beauty that makes us who we are.

It isn't until we are awake and dreaming that we start living.

Do you remember the time ... ?

One recurring topic that consistently pops up is regret. Like anyone, I sometimes think of regret and any instances that cause this feeling. Of course, if we knew the results of decisions prior to making them, we could eliminate that; however, I know that isn't how life works. I have begun to decipher the term "regret" and its complexities so that it can work in my favor. The decisions made at the time of your impasse must be ones that you accept, regardless of the outcome. Whether it works out in your favor or not, you must be content with the results.

The critical moment in all of this is the exact moment before you make up your mind and make your choice. This is the step that can change your life forever, so it's important you think through it properly. As for the outcomes, days, weeks, months or years later, realize that you must be okay regardless of how they played out. From the good results to the ones that are not in your favor, you must remain humble. To appreciate or know winning you must equate your life with some loss. Never in the history of mankind has there been anyone who has endured only wins. Now, for your wins, remain humble and congratulate yourself on making the right decision. For your losses, contest the loss and the reason behind it, but only for your learning. Remain humble and know that with every loss comes a lesson (the hidden silver lining).

Memory Remembrance

At times we suffer from "memory remembrance," which I define as "looking back at certain times in life and regretting not doing more." In truth, that time is long gone, and we can't do anything to get it back. It would be a waste of time for us to think back and regret the things we didn't do. It's simply too late. What we can do, however, is live in the present and allow ourselves the ability to learn from this feeling of regret, learning to allow ourselves the ability to recognize and to change our now so that our future can be about fulfillment and satisfaction.

We forget the gift of living in the moment (consider my story about the Dominican with my friends). If life has taught me anything, it's to give all that you can in the moment, and I mean that wholeheartedly. If you are encased in emotions of love, allow love to radiate with no limits. Allow your ego and pride to leave and allow your vulnerability to shine through. This moment that you give love may never be repeated. It may never have the same affect again, and the person receiving it may not be around.

If it is time, allow yourself within the realms of reality to give your time to those around you whom you believe deserve it. Time spent with your loved ones or someone you care for can create so many new opportunities in life for both of you.

These opportunities are not tangible but rather emotional, spiritual, and soulful ones that can change someone's life.

A week before the accident my brother had messaged me asking me to go out and eat. It was a Sunday. We ended up going to Denny's all-day breakfast, and I remember sitting down with him and ordering almost everything we wanted. I remember thinking to myself at that time that the happiness I was a part of was amazing. We ate our life away that night and drank so much chocolate milk that we spent the following days hugging the toilet!! That moment will remain with me for the rest of my life and will be one that I can cherish forever. The Sunday before the accident, he messaged me again to go out and eat, and I told him I was busy working on a project and needed to finish up all the details by Monday.

I had allowed work to get in the way of my family, and as much as I cherished the first outing with him, I heavily regretted not going out the second time. What I have learned from this is that I must live in the now and cherish every moment as if it were the last. If you ask anyone around me, they'll tell you that I really do try to be on good terms and to apologize if something is off. If we are enjoying a moment, I try to enjoy it and never allow work to get in the way. It all stems from that night I said no to my brother.

When it comes to these instances, do what you think is right and live with the consequences. I only share who I am and what I believe to be the right way of going about it. I hope that we can all be a little more open and loving towards each other, as it gets us so much further in life. If you are witnessing your friends' success, show them love and celebrate them. Chances are you're celebrating yourself too, and by doing this, you're spreading love towards others.

Life is difficult, but so are your choices.

Life isn't easy, but it's beautiful. Things get better with time if we allow time, time. Too many people run away from their emotions and block out feelings. Confrontation may not be their strong suit now, but sooner or later, life's problems will appear right in front of them. If we run away from all that bothers us, does that not make us weak? We all do it, but it's important to realize that if we allow the confrontation to occur today, we take away from the problem in the future. That is peace. Today we may struggle, but tomorrow we live peacefully.

In conclusion, I want you to know that the image of who you are can only be seen in the third person. Don't be too harsh with yourself. Every human being we have encountered holds a different image of us. The one image that does not change is the self-image, the one that you are, the one that you are born with, and the one that you remain faithful to. Don't change unless it's for the greater good and from a place that you know you want to.

Remain true to your core beliefs and allow the mercy of life to enter. Do not be too hard with your emotions, and please do not block out any energy that you know should flow right through you. If you are dealing with pain, allow the pain to happen. Cry it out, yell it out, or scream it out, but whatever you do, do not hold it in. if you feel the need to see a therapist, do so. There is no shame in getting help to better yourself. If you feel like you need to talk, reach out to someone that you are comfortable with, and let them know you are coming from a vulnerable place. For a man, that is very hard to do, but the first step towards your betterment is realizing that you need to. Do not remain stagnant; we are not mean to stay comfortable as humans. We must always evolve, and that may not mean just physically, but emotionally and spiritually. Find out what makes you happy and do that one thing with passion. If there is one thing that you can do a day that will put a smile on your face, do it.

If this book has helped you in the slightest, I have succeeded. If there is a 1% chance that I have been able to help change something in your life for the better, then I have completed my mission. Please relate to my story and use me as a steppingstone to realize that things get better with time. If we live today with the lessons of the past and look toward the future, we can live a fulfilled life.

Dedication

To Shadi, forever my brother.

Thank you for giving me the greatest lesson of life: love.